Praise for *The Yes Brain*

"Easily assimilated and informative, the book will help adults enable children to lead physically and emotionally satisfying and well-rounded lives filled with purpose and meaningful relationships. Edifying, easy-to-understand scientific research that shows the benefits that accrue when a child is encouraged to be inquisitive, spirited, and intrepid."   —*Kirkus Reviews*

"This unique and exciting book shows us how to help children embrace life with all of its challenges and thrive in the modern world. Integrating research from social development, clinical psychology, and neuroscience, it's a veritable treasure chest of parenting insights and techniques."   —Carol S. Dweck, Ph.D., author of *Mindset*

"In today's busy, competitive culture, allowing our children the space to be themselves is more important than ever. This book provides an escape hatch from the high-stakes mindset. It's a parent's guide to ensuring health, happiness, and genuine success—a blueprint for ...ng confident, creative kids in a fear-based world. It's never too late to implement the science-based strategies that Daniel J. Siegel and Tina Payne Bryson share."

"Bottom line: Every parent wants to raise a strong-minded, resilient, caring child. We just don't know exactly how; we open our mouths and we sing our parents' tired refrain, 'No . . . no . . . no.' In *The Yes Brain*, Siegel and Bryson teach us how to cultivate a receptive, curious brain in our children. I have never read a better, clearer explanation of the impact parenting can have on a child's brain and personality."

"Today's parents find their children's behavior mystifying. 'I never would have spoken that way to—or refused to cooperate with—my parents!' Using refreshingly clear explanations of neuroscience and child development, coupled with practical, straightforward guidance, *The Yes Brain* arrives just in time! Siegel and Bryson lead parents and children out of puzzling impasses and into mutual understanding and appreciation. The book gives them the tools and courage needed to face the challenges of our rapidly changing world."

"In the flurry of activity that makes up our day-to-day parenting lives, it is easy to lose sight of the big picture: We aren't just raising children; we're raising adults. *The Yes Brain* offers clear strategies for fostering balance, empathy, and self-regulation in our children to not only help them manage today's bumps and tumbles, but to nurture in them the resources that will allow them to enjoy happy, healthy grown-up lives. An invaluable resource that I'll be recommending to parents for years to come!"

—Susan Stiffelman, MFT, author of
Parenting Without Power Struggles

BY DANIEL J. SIEGEL, M.D., AND TINA PAYNE BRYSON, PH.D.

The Whole-Brain Child

No-Drama Discipline

The Yes Brain

The Yes Brain

The Yes Brain

HOW TO CULTIVATE COURAGE, CURIOSITY, AND RESILIENCE IN YOUR CHILD

Daniel J. Siegel, M.D., and Tina Payne Bryson, Ph.D.

Bantam New York

2019 Bantam Books Trade Paperback Edition

Published in the United States by Bantam Books, an imprint of Random House, a division of Penguin Random House LLC, New York.

BANTAM BOOKS and the HOUSE colophon are registered trademarks of Penguin Random House LLC.

Originally published in hardcover in the United States by Bantam Books, an imprint of Random House, a division of Penguin Random House LLC, in 2018.

The section entitled "Balance and the Overscheduled Child" on pages 59–61 was adapted from articles that Tina Payne Bryson wrote for www.mom.me and any direct quotes are reprinted with permission.

Illustrations by Tuesday Mourning

LIBRARY OF CONGRESS CATALOGING-IN-PUBLICATION DATA
Names: Siegel, Daniel J., author. | Bryson, Tina Payne, author.
Title: The yes brain: how to cultivate courage, curiosity, and resilience in your child / Daniel J. Siegel, M.D. and Tina Payne Bryson, Ph.D.
Description: New York: Bantam, 2018.
Identifiers: LCCN 2017037802 | ISBN 9780399594687 (trade paperback) | ISBN 9780399594670 (ebook)
Subjects: LCSH: Resilience (Personality trait) in children. | Child rearing. | Parenting. | BISAC: FAMILY & RELATIONSHIPS / Parenting / General. | PSYCHOLOGY / Developmental / Child.
Classification: LCC BF723.R46 S54 2018 | DDC 155.4/1824—dc23
LC record available at https://lccn.loc.gov/2017037802

Printed in the United States of America on acid-free paper

randomhousebooks.com

9 8 7 6 5

Series book design by Liz Cosgrove

To Alex and Maddi, my greatest teachers of a Yes Brain approach to life

—DJS

To Ben, Luke, and JP: I delight in you and I marvel at the light you bring to the world.

—TPB

I'm not afraid of storms, for I'm learning how to sail my ship.

—Louisa May Alcott, *Little Women*

WELCOME

"There's so much I want for my kids: happiness, emotional strength, academic success, social skills, a strong sense of self, and more. It's hard to know where to even start. What characteristics are most important to focus on to help them live happy, meaningful lives?"

We get some version of this question everywhere we go. Parents want to help their kids become people who can handle themselves well and make good decisions, even when life is challenging. They want them to care for others but also know how to stand up for themselves. They want them to be independent and also enjoy mutually rewarding relationships. They want them to avoid melting down when things don't go their way.

Whew! That's quite a list, and it can put a lot of pressure on us as parents (or as professionals who work with kids). So where should we focus our attention?

The book you're holding is our attempt to offer a response to that question. The essential idea is that parents can help children develop a Yes Brain, which produces four key characteristics:

Balance: the ability to manage emotions and behavior, so kids are less likely to flip their lids and lose control;

Resilience: the ability to bounce back when life's inevitable
problems and struggles arise;

Insight: the ability to look within and understand themselves,
then use what they learn to make good decisions and be
more in control of their lives;

Empathy: the ability to understand the perspective of another,
then care enough to take action to make things better
when appropriate.

In the pages that follow, we'll introduce you to the Yes Brain and
discuss practical ways you can nurture these qualities in your children and teach them these important life skills. You really can help
your kids become more emotionally balanced, more resilient in the
face of struggles, more insightful when it comes to understanding
themselves, and more empathic and caring toward others.

We couldn't be more excited to share this science-inspired approach with you. Come with us, and enjoy the journey of learning
about the Yes Brain.

Dan and Tina

CONTENTS

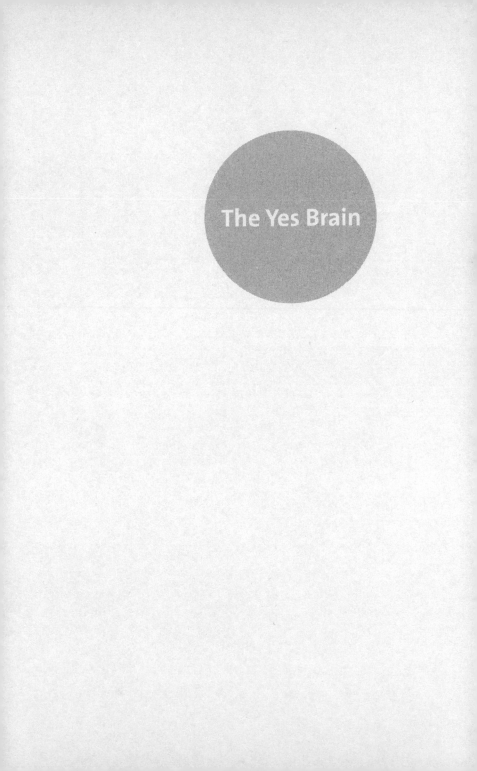

The Yes Brain

CHAPTER 1

The Yes Brain: An Introduction

This book is about helping kids say yes to the world. It's about encouraging them to open their minds to new challenges, to new opportunities, to who they already are and all they can become. It's about giving them a Yes Brain.

If you've heard Dan speak, you may have participated in an exercise where he asks his audience to close their eyes and pay attention to their bodily and emotional responses when he repeats a particular word. He begins by somewhat harshly saying "no" over and over again. He repeats it seven times, then switches to "yes," which he says much more gently, again and again. He then asks the audience members to open their eyes and describe what they experienced. They report that the "no" portion of the exercise left them feeling shut down, upset, tense, and defensive, whereas when Dan repeated the affirming "yes," they felt open, calm, relaxed, and lighter. The muscles of their face and vocal cords relaxed, their breathing and heart rate normalized, and they became more open, as opposed to restricted or insecure or oppositional. (Feel free to close your eyes now and try the exercise for yourself. Maybe enlist the help of a relative or friend.

Notice what goes on in your body as you repeatedly hear the word "no," and then "yes.")

These two different responses—the "yes" response and the "no" response—give you an idea of what we mean when we talk about a Yes Brain, as well as its opposite, a No Brain. If you expand that and think about it as an overall outlook on life, a No Brain leaves you feeling *reactive* when you interact with people, which makes it nearly impossible to listen, make good decisions, or connect with and care for another person. A focus on survival and self-defense kicks into gear, leaving you feeling guarded and shut down when it comes to interacting with the world and learning new lessons. Your nervous system initiates its reactive fight-flight-freeze-or-faint response: fight means lashing out, flight means escaping, freeze means temporarily immobilizing yourself, and faint means collapsing and feeling utterly helpless. Any of these four reactive responses to threat can become triggered, preventing you from being open, connecting to others, and offering flexible responses. That's the reactive No Brain state.

The Yes Brain, in contrast, emerges from different circuits in the brain that become activated and lead to *receptivity* rather than reactivity. Scientists use the term "social engagement system" to refer to the set of neural circuits that help us connect openly with others—and even our own inner experience. As a result of receptivity and an active social engagement system, we feel much more capable of addressing challenges in a strong, clear, and flexible way. In this Yes Brain state, we open ourselves to a sense of equanimity and harmony, allowing us to absorb, assimilate, and learn from new information.

This Yes Brain mindset is what we want for our kids, so that they learn to view obstacles and new experiences not as paralyzing impediments but simply as challenges to be faced and overcome and learned from. When kids work from a Yes Brain mentality, they're more flexible, more open to compromise, more willing to take chances and explore. They're more curious and imaginative, less worried about making mistakes. They're also less rigid and stubborn, which makes them better at relationships and more adaptable and resilient when it comes to handling adversity. They understand themselves and work from a clear internal compass that directs their decisions as well as the way they treat others. Guided by their Yes Brain, they do more, learn more, and become more. They say yes to the

WHAT A YES BRAIN LOOKS LIKE

world from a place of emotional equilibrium, welcoming all that life offers—even when circumstances don't go their way.

Our opening message to you is a thrilling one: you have the power to promote this type of flexibility, receptivity, and resilience in your children. This is what we mean by mental strength—giving your kids a strong mind. Not by making them attend a lecture series on grit and curiosity, or by initiating lots of long, intense, stare-into-each-other's-eyes conversations. In fact, your everyday interactions with your children are all you need. Simply by keeping in mind the Yes Brain principles and lessons we'll show you in the coming pages, you can use the time you spend with your kids—while driving to school, eating dinner, playing together, or even arguing with them—to influence the way they respond to their circumstances and interact with the people around them.

That's because a Yes Brain is more than just a mindset or an approach to the world. It's that, definitely. And as such, it gives your child an internal guide to help him or her face life's challenges with security and enthusiasm. It's the basis of being strong from the inside out. But a Yes Brain is also a neurological state that emerges when the brain is engaged in certain ways. By understanding a few basic details about brain development, you can help create an environment that provides opportunities that will foster a Yes Brain in your kids.

As we'll explain below, the Yes Brain is created by neural activity that involves a particular region of the brain called the prefrontal cortex, an area that links many regions with one another, handles higher-order thinking, and facilitates curiosity, resilience, compassion, insight, open-mindedness, problem-solving, and even morality. Kids can learn to increasingly access and pay attention to the functions of this part of the brain as they grow and develop. In other words, you can teach your kids how to grow this important neural area that supports mental strength. As a result, they can control their emotions and bodies better, while also listening more carefully to their inner promptings and being more fully themselves. That's what we're talking about when we discuss the Yes Brain: a neurological state that helps children (and adults) approach the world with openness, resilience, empathy, and authenticity.

A No Brain, in contrast, emerges less from the interconnecting prefrontal cortex and more from a less integrated brain state that involves the activity of lower, more primitive regions of the brain. This No Brain state is how we respond to a threat or get ready for an impending attack. As a result, it's intensely reactive, defensively worrying that it might make a mistake or that curiosity might lead to some kind of trouble. And this state can go on the offense, too, pushing back on new knowledge and fighting off input from others. Attacking and rejecting are two ways the No Brain deals with the world. The No Brain's outlook on the world is one of stubbornness, anxiety, competition, and threat, leaving it much less capable of handling difficult situations or achieving a clear understanding of self or others.

Kids who approach the world from a No Brain state are at the mercy of their circumstances and their feelings. They get stuck in their emotions, unable to shift them, and they complain about their realities rather than finding healthy ways to respond to them. They worry, often obsessively, about facing something new or making a mistake, rather than making decisions in a Yes Brain spirit of openness and curiosity. Stubbornness often rules the day in a No Brain state.

Does any of that sound similar to your situation at home? If you have kids, it probably does. The truth is, we all get into No Brain states—kids and adults alike. Becoming rigid and/or reactive from time to time is something we can't completely avoid. But we *can* understand it. Then we can learn ways to help our kids return more quickly to a Yes Brain state when they leave it. And more important, we can give them the tools to do so themselves. Young children will work from a No Brain state more often than older children and adults. A seemingly omnipresent No Brain is typical and developmentally appropriate for a three-year-old—like when she cries with fury because her harmonica got wet, even though *she's* the one who threw it in the sink full of water! But over time, and as development unfolds, we can support our kids in developing the ability to regulate

WHAT A NO BRAIN LOOKS LIKE

themselves, bounce back from difficulties, understand their own experiences, and be thoughtful of others. Then, more and more, the no becomes a yes.

Think about that right now, for just a moment. How would life at your house change if your kids were better at responding to everyday situations—conflict with siblings, turning off electronics, following directions, homework struggles, bedtime battles—from a Yes Brain instead of reacting from a No Brain? What would be different if they were less rigid and stubborn and they could better regulate themselves when things don't go their way? What if they welcomed new experiences instead of fearing them? What if they could be clearer about their own feelings, and more caring and empathic toward others? How much happier would they be? How much happier and more peaceful would the whole family be?

That's what this book is about: helping develop a Yes Brain in your kids by giving them the space, the opportunity, and the tools to develop into people who openly engage with their world and become fully and authentically themselves. This is how we help children develop mental strength and resilience.

How would life at your house change if your kids were able to respond to everyday situations from a Yes Brain instead of reacting from a No Brain?

Nurturing a Yes Brain Is Not About Being Permissive

Let us be clear from the outset about what the Yes Brain is not. The Yes Brain is *not* about telling kids yes all the time. It's not about being permissive, or giving in, or protecting them from disappointment, or rescuing them from difficult situations. Nor is it about creating a compliant child who robotically minds his parents without thinking for himself. Instead, it's about helping kids begin to realize who they are and who they are becoming, and that they can overcome disappointment and defeat and choose a life full of connection and meaning. Chapters 2 and 3 especially will discuss the importance of allowing children to understand that frustrations and setbacks are an inherent part of life—and supporting them while they learn that lesson.

After all, the result of a Yes Brain is not a person who is happy all

The Yes Brain is not at all about telling kids yes all the time. It's not about being permissive, or giving in, or protecting them from disappointment, or rescuing them from difficult situations. Instead, it's about helping them begin to realize who they are and who they are becoming, and that they can overcome disappointment and defeat and choose a life full of connection and meaning.

the time or who never experiences any problems or negative feelings. That's not the point at all. It's not the goal of life, nor is it possible. The Yes Brain leads not to some sort of perfection or paradise, but to the ability to find joy and meaning even in the midst of life's challenges. It allows a person to feel grounded and understand themselves, to flexibly learn and adapt, and to live with a sense of purpose. It leads them not only to survive difficult situations, but to emerge from them stronger and wiser. That's how they can develop meaning in their lives. From their Yes Brain they're also able to engage with their inner life, with others, and with the world. That's what we mean by having a life of connection and knowing who we are.

When kids and adolescents also develop the ability for equanimity—for learning the skill of returning to a Yes Brain state after being in No Brain mode—we've given them an important component of resilience. The ancient Greeks had a term for this kind of happiness composed of meaning, connection, and peaceful contentedness. They called it *eudaimonia*, and it's one of the most empowering and lasting gifts we can give our children. It helps create the kind of successful life we can prepare our kids for if we allow them to mature into their own individual identities while supporting them and building skills along the way. And, of course, by working on our own Yes Brain.

Let's face it: in many ways kids are growing up in a No Brain world. Think about a traditional school day, full of rules and regulations, standardized tests, rote memorization, and one-size-fits-all discipline techniques. Whew! And they have to deal with that six hours a day, five days a week, for nine months of the year? Yikes. On top of that, consider the oh-so-packed schedules so many of us impose on them, full of "enrichment" classes and tutoring and other activities that leave them staying up late and losing sleep because they have to get their homework done because they couldn't do it during the daylight hours since they were so busy being "enriched." When we add to this how compelling digital media has become, with auditory and visual stimuli capturing our kids' attention around the clock with a temporary pleasure the Greeks called *hedonia*, we can realize that cultivating a Yes Brain is especially important in these modern times to empower our kids with true and lasting happiness, with the *eudaimonia* of meaning, connection, and equanimity.

These digital distractions and busy schedules are often experiences that fail to ignite—and at times even undermine—Yes Brain thought. Some of them may actually offer enriching experiences, and some may be necessary evils (although we're not convinced how necessary certain commonly accepted educational practices really are, as evidenced by the inspirational work being done all over the country and the world by educators who are challenging the status quo in the areas of homework, class schedules, and discipline). Yes, of course kids need to learn about managing routines, following a calendar, and completing tasks that aren't necessarily pleasant or fun. You'll hear us endorse that idea throughout the book. Our main point here is simply that when you consider how many of a child's waking hours are spent doing No Brain work or engaged in No Brain activities, it becomes that much more important that we strive to offer them Yes Brain interactions whenever we possibly can. We want to make home a place where a "yes" approach is consistently emphasized and prioritized.

When you consider how many of a child's waking hours are spent doing No Brain work and No Brain activities, it becomes that much more important that we strive to offer them Yes Brain interactions whenever we possibly can.

One other point about what the Yes

Brain is *not*: it's not about putting more pressure on parents to be perfect or to avoid ever messing up with their children. In fact, the idea here is to relax a bit. Just as your kids don't have to be perfect, neither do you. Cut yourself some slack. Be as emotionally present for your kids as you possibly can, then allow development to happen, supporting them along the way.

If you know our books *The Whole-Brain Child* and *No-Drama Discipline*, you'll immediately see how *The Yes Brain* is a continuation and extension of what we've said before. All three books focus on the conviction that our children's brains—and therefore their lives—are significantly impacted by their experiences, including how we communicate with them, what we model for them, and what kinds of relationships we build with them. In *The Whole-Brain Child* we explained the importance of intentionally promoting integration in our kids' brains and relationships, so they can be both fully themselves and also meaningfully connected with the people around them. In *No-Drama Discipline* we focused on seeing the mind behind our children's behavior, on peeling back the layers of their actions and understanding that discipline issues are opportunities to teach and build skills.

Here we take those concepts a step further and apply them to the question of what kind of overall experience with the world you want your kids to enjoy. Our focus in the coming pages is to give you new ways to think about and develop the Yes Brain in each individual child, so that you can fan the flame of her unique inner spark and help it grow and spread as it illuminates and bolsters her sense of self and the world around her. We'll introduce you to some of the latest, cutting-edge science and research on the brain and help you apply that information in your relationship with your child. While some of what we show you in these pages may mean a shift in how you think and what you do as a parent, and some of it will indeed require some practice, there's plenty that you can begin using right now, today, to make a difference in your child's development and in the relationship you two share. Simply understanding a few Yes Brain fundamentals will help you survive the daily, here-and-now challenges you face as a parent—the meltdowns, the battles over screen time and bedtime, the fear of failure and new experiences, the homework freak-outs, the rigid perfectionism, the stubbornness, the sibling conflict—while also helping you build long-lasting skills in your kids that will empower them to lead rich, meaningful lives.

By the way, we'll be addressing parents throughout, but everything we say here is for anyone who loves and cares for the kids in their lives. That goes for grandparents, teachers, therapists, coaches, and anyone else tasked with the immense and joyful responsibility of helping children grow into the fullness of themselves. We're grateful that there are so many adults working together to love and guide the children in their lives, and to help introduce them to the fundamentals of the Yes Brain.

The Integrated, "Plastic" Brain

What we've said so far, and what we'll discuss in the remainder of the book, is based on the latest research about the brain. The scientific lens through which we view these parental challenges is interpersonal neurobiology (IPNB), a multidisciplinary view drawing on research from around the world. Dan is the founding editor of the Norton Series on Interpersonal Neurobiology, an extensive professional library of more than fifty titles with tens of thousands of scientific references, so if you're as nerdy as we are and want to "geek out" on the hard-core science behind these ideas, there's nowhere better to go than that series. But you don't have to be a neurobiologist to understand some IPNB basics that can benefit your relationship with your child immediately.

The focus of interpersonal neurobiology is just what you'd expect: neurobiology, from an interpersonal perspective. Put simply, IPNB looks at how our mind, our brain, and our relationships interact to shape who we are. You can think of it as the "triangle of well-being." IPNB studies connections *within* a person's brain, as well as *between* the brains of different individuals that emerge in their relationships with one another.

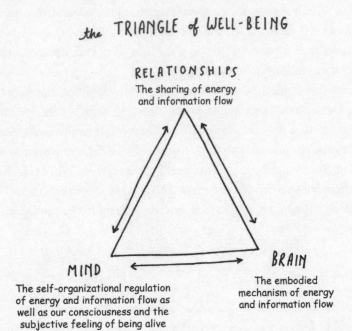

the TRIANGLE *of* WELL-BEING

RELATIONSHIPS
The sharing of energy
and information flow

MIND
The self-organizational regulation
of energy and information flow as
well as our consciousness and the
subjective feeling of being alive

BRAIN
The embodied
mechanism of energy
and information flow

Perhaps the key concept that guides IPNB is *integration*, which describes what happens when differentiated parts work together as a coordinated whole. The brain is made up of many parts, each with different functions: the left and right hemispheres; the higher and lower parts of the brain; sensory neurons, memory centers, and various other circuitry in charge of functions such as language, emotion, and motor control; and on and on. These different parts of the brain have their own responsibilities, their own jobs to do. And when they work together as a team, as a coordinated whole, the brain becomes integrated, so it can accomplish more and be much more effective than it could if its parts were working by themselves. That's why we've talked so much over the years about whole-brain parenting: we want to help kids develop and integrate their whole brains, so that different regions of the brain become more connected, both structurally (meaning the way they physically connect via neurons) and functionally (meaning the way they work, or function, together). Both structural and functional integration are key to a person's overall well-being.

The most recent neuroscientific research supports the importance of an integrated brain. You may have heard about the Human Connectome Project, the NIH-supported study that gathered biologists, physicians, computer scientists, and physicists for an enormous study of the human brain. One of the key findings of the project, which examined more than twelve hundred healthy human brains, is especially pertinent to what we're saying here. When you look at all the positive goals a person hopes for in life—happiness, bodily and mental health, academic and career success, relational satisfaction, and so on—the number one predictor for these positive outcomes is an integrated brain, revealed in how interconnected the connectome is, meaning how well the differentiated areas of the brain are linked to one another.

In other words, if you want to help your child grow into a person who's able to live meaningfully and find success throughout his life, there's virtually nothing more important than helping integrate his or her brain. We've written a great deal about practical ways to do this, and it's also what much of this book is about. As a parent—or as a grandparent, teacher, or other caregiver—you have the opportunity to give the child you love experiences that create these important connections in his brain. All kids are different, and there's no "silver bullet" that addresses every situation, but with effort and intentionality you can create a space in your child's life that will help connect the different regions of his brain, both structurally and functionally, so those regions can communicate and collaborate with one another and produce these positive outcomes.

If you want to help your child grow into a person who's able to live meaningfully and find success throughout his life, there's virtually nothing more important than helping integrate his brain.

A Yes Brain is the state of integrated brain functioning that promotes the growth of integrated structural connections in the brain itself. When you encourage a Yes Brain in your interactions with your child, you are empowering her to grow a more integrated brain.

It's easy to understand why integration is so important. We use the acronym FACES to describe the characteristics of an integrated brain.

The FACES of an Integrated Brain

F LEXIBLE

A DAPTIVE

C OHERENT

E NERGIZED

S TABLE

An interconnected, integrated brain, in which its many parts are working together as a coordinated and balanced whole, is more flexible, adaptive, coherent, energized, and stable. As a result, a child with an integrated brain will be better at handling herself when things don't go her way. Instead of responding to the world from a position of *reactivity*, where she is at the mercy of her surroundings and her emotions, she's more able to work from an attitude of *receptivity*, willing and able to *decide* how she wants to respond to various situations and challenges. This is how children build self-understanding and an internal compass to guide them, with intrinsic goals and inner drive. That's a Yes Brain mentality, and you can see why it allows kids to make better decisions, relate better to others, and understand themselves more fully.

One key reason guiding the growth of higher degrees of integration is possible is that the brain is plastic, or moldable, and changes based on our experiences. This concept is known as neuroplasticity, and it refers to the fact that it's not just a person's *mind*, or way of thinking, that changes throughout life. Of course that happens, too, but neuroplasticity is about much more than that. The actual physical architecture of the brain adapts to new information, reorganizing itself and creating new neural pathways based on what a person sees, hears, touches, thinks about, practices, and so on. Anything we give attention to, anything we emphasize in our experiences and interactions, creates new linking connections in the brain. Where attention goes, neurons fire. And where neurons fire, they wire, or join together.

WHERE ATTENTION GOES NEURAL FIRING FLOWS and NEURAL CONNECTION GROWS

Neuroplasticity leads to some very interesting questions for parents in terms of what kinds of experiences they create for their children. Since parents have the ability, with where and how they draw their kids' attention, to build and strengthen important connections in their children's brains, it's crucial that parents think about those experiences, and about what kinds of connections they are helping wire in those young brains. Where attention goes, neurons fire. With a Yes Brain state, when neurons fire, they wire in constructive ways, changing and integrating the brain. So when you're reading with your child and ask, "Why do you think that made the little girl sad?" you are giving him a chance to build and strengthen the empathy and social engagement circuitry in his brain. Simply because you gave attention to that particular emotion, you are building the circuitry of self-understanding. Or when you tell jokes and riddles, you're giving attention to humor and logic, helping develop those aspects of your child's self. In the same way, exposing your child to toxic shame and excessive criticism, either from you or from a teacher or coach or someone else, will lay neural pathways that will affect her sense of self. This No Brain state created in interaction with you can also grow the brain—but now it is not growing in an integrated way.

The choice is up to you: No Brain or Yes Brain? Just as a gardener uses a rake, or a doctor a stethoscope, a parent can use the tool of attention to help develop and link important parts of a child's brain. That's how you can guide your child's growth toward integration.

Since parents have the ability, with where and how they draw their kids' attention, to build and strengthen important connections in their children's brains, it's crucial that parents think about those experiences, and about what kinds of connections they are helping wire in those young brains.

Likewise, when we neglect certain parts of our child's development, those parts of their brains can be "pruned"—they can be underdeveloped and even wither and die. That means that if kids don't receive certain experiences, or their attention isn't ever brought to certain information, they can lose access to those skills, especially through the process of adolescence. If, for example, your child never hears about generosity and giving, the part of her brain responsible for those functions can fail to develop fully. The same applies if she isn't provided with free time to play and be curious and explore. Those neurons will fail to fire, and the necessary integration that leads to thriving won't occur in the same way. Some of these skills may be attainable later in life with energy and effort, but it's best to offer such brain-developing experiences when they first can grow in childhood and adolescence. As we'll explain again and again throughout the book, what you do and don't value, and what you do and don't give attention to, will impact who your child becomes.

Other factors, such as temperament and various inborn variables, are obviously important as well when it comes to shaping the development of the brain's function and structure. Genes can play a major role in shaping the brain and therefore the behavior of individual children. But we also significantly impact our kids through the experiences we facilitate, even in the face of inborn differences that are beyond our control. What this means is that tuning in to your particular child to find the kinds of experiences that she needs and to help focus her attention in ways that suit her individual temperament are important ways that you can help shape further brain growth. Experience shapes the growth of connections in the brain—in childhood, in adolescence, and throughout our adult lives!

The Four Fundamentals of the Yes Brain

If you've read our other books, you know that we talk a lot about building what we call the *upstairs brain*. The brain is obviously exceptionally complex, so one way we've simplified this particular concept is by comparing a child's developing brain to a house under construction, with both a downstairs and an upstairs. The bottom floor represents the more primitive parts of the brain—the brainstem and limbic region—which exist in the lower portion of the brain, ranging from the top of the neck to the bridge of the nose. We call this the *downstairs brain*, and it's responsible for our most fundamental neural and mental operations, including strong emotions, instincts, and basic functions such as digestion and breathing. The downstairs brain operates extremely quickly, largely without our even being aware that it's doing its work. It will often cause us to be reactive in a certain situation, and to act before thinking, since downstairs is where these instinctual, lower-order, often automatic processes take place.

At birth, the downstairs part of the brain is fairly well developed. The upstairs brain, on the other hand, is the part of the house that's still under major construction, and it's in charge of more complex thinking, emotional, and relational skills. It is made up of the cerebral cortex, which is the outermost layer of the brain, directly behind the forehead and continuing toward the back of the head, like a half dome covering the downstairs brain beneath it. The upstairs brain allows us to plan ahead, consider consequences, solve difficult problems, consider various perspectives, and perform other sophisticated cognitive activities associated with executive function. Much, but by no means all, of what we often experience in our day-to-day awareness is an outcome of the higher mental processes of our upstairs brain.

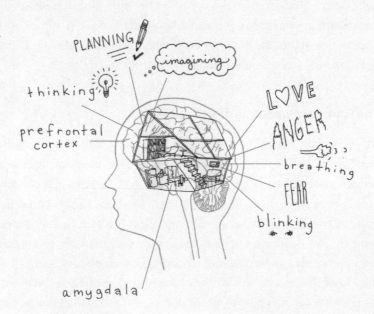

The upstairs brain takes time to evolve as a child grows and matures. In fact, not until a person reaches his mid-twenties will the construction of the upstairs brain be complete. If you want a single reason to be patient with your child when he's melting down or being unreasonable in some way, this is it: his brain isn't fully formed yet, and he is, at least at times, literally incapable of controlling his emotions and body. He's operating from his downstairs, primitive, reptilian brain in those moments. That's where you, as the parent, come in. One of your main jobs as the caretaker of this child is to nurture and love him *while* you help build and strengthen his upstairs brain. In a way, you're his external upstairs brain until his is well developed. Along the way, you can help mold your child's plastic brain, integrating it by offering Yes Brain experiences that develop the various functions of the upstairs brain and help it balance the functions of the downstairs brain.

It makes sense, doesn't it, that you'd want to help develop the part of your child that allows her to be a reasonable, caring, resilient, responsible individual? That's what the upstairs brain does. To be more specific, there's one section of the upstairs brain, the prefrontal cortex (PFC), that's responsible for practically all of the behaviors we expect from a mature and caring human being with an active Yes Brain: flexibility and adaptability, sound decision making and planning, regulation of emotions and body, personal insight, empathy, and morality. These are the behaviors that result from a fully formed, highly functioning PFC, and they represent the essence of social and emotional intelligence. When a person's PFC is doing its job, when integration is created, that person feels happy and connected and at home in the world. That's what creates the kind of happiness of *eudaimonia*, enabling a life of meaning, connection, and equanimity. That person views life from the perspective of a Yes Brain.

As you'll see in the coming chapters, we've taken this list of behaviors that emerge from an integrated PFC and simplified it into what we call the Four Fundamentals of the Yes Brain:

When the PFC and related areas are engaged and doing their job, the Yes Brain emerges as we allow and encourage a child to grow and develop into who she is. Taking care always to allow for and embrace her individual temperament and identity, we then teach the skills and abilities that can help her along the way. These four fundamentals are the offshoots that emanate from an engaged and integrated upstairs brain.

For instance, when we see that the child is having trouble handling big emotions, we help her build the skill of balance, which is all about regulating her emotions and body and making good decisions, even when she's upset. Or if she tends to have a hard time being persistent when facing difficult circumstances, we can work with her on being more resilient. Having developed greater balance and stronger resilience, she's more prepared to develop the insight necessary to genuinely understand herself and her emotions, meaning she can truly *decide* what she cares about and who she wants to be. That's the core of what we're calling an internal compass. Then the final Yes Brain fundamental is empathy, where she takes these strengths and insights about herself and uses them to better understand and care for herself and others, and to act in moral and ethical ways. As we'll explain in Chapter 5, we are using the general term "empathy" here with its wide range of scientific meanings, including feeling another's feelings (emotional resonance), imagining another's point of view (perspective-taking), understanding another (cognitive empathy), sharing another's happiness (empathic joy), and kind, caring concern with an interest in helping (compassionate empathy).

All of the four fundamentals are skills to be learned, and each successive step toward a Yes Brain worldview moves her closer to living a life full of balance, resilience, insight, and empathy.

Notice, then, that the process is cyclical. A Yes Brain leads to greater balance, resilience, insight, and empathy in a child. Then, as we work to encourage and promote these fundamentals, they further reinforce a Yes Brain approach to the world, which then leads, once again, to even more balance, resilience, insight, and empathy. It's a recurring, growth-oriented process leading to better and better outcomes in our children. In many ways, this reveals a fascinating finding from science: integration creates more integration. A Yes Brain interaction encourages more Yes Brain states to emerge. When, in your role as a parent, you learn to become aware of these skills and to develop a Yes Brain state in yourself, you may be happily surprised to find, as we and so many others we work with do, that this new skill positively reinforces itself. (You may have already realized that and even be thinking, "Oh, Dan and Tina, that's a no-brainer." But we would say that this is a Yes-Brainer!)

Remaining mindful of the idea that the PFC and the rest of the upstairs brain are still under construction, we can therefore work to be patient, careful not to expect more than kids are capable of in terms of behavior and perspective. But by offering your kids experiences that encourage them to be more balanced, resilient, insightful, and empathic, you'll be growing and strengthening and supporting their upstairs brain, and preparing them for true lifelong success. You'll help them develop a strong Yes Brain, and all the benefits that come with it.

Remember, each of the four fundamentals is a skill that your child can develop with practice and your guidance. While some kids are more naturally balanced, resilient, insightful, or empathic, each child's brain is also plastic and able to grow and develop based on the integrating experiences the child undergoes. So we'll introduce you to basic information about each of the fundamentals, as well as practical steps you can take to help promote and develop that particular skill in your child's life.

Encouraging a Yes Brain offers significant advantages, both short-term and long-term. The most immediate benefit is that your job as a parent will get easier. A child who has developed a more robust ability to access his Yes Brain will not only be happier and more interested in the world; he'll also be more flexible and easier to work with, since reactivity will be replaced with receptivity (more about this soon). So that's the day-to-day benefit of giving your child the skill of activating a Yes Brain: a more peaceful and easygoing child and a stronger parent-child relationship. The long-term benefit is that you'll be building and integrating your child's upstairs brain and teaching him skills he'll use throughout adolescence and adulthood. After all, these four fundamentals are the *eudaimonia* touchstones of a healthy, happy, authentic life.

At the end of each chapter you'll find two sections designed to give you more ways to put the chapter's ideas into practice. The first, "Yes Brain Kids," is a cartoon strip written to help you discuss the ideas

The most immediate benefit of encouraging a Yes Brain in your kids is that your job as a parent will get easier. The long-term benefit is that you'll be building and integrating their upstairs brain and teaching them skills they'll use throughout adolescence and adulthood.

of that particular fundamental with your child. We've used this approach in other books and have consistently heard from parents, teachers, and clinicians how helpful it is when they can not only digest the information themselves but teach it to kids as well. For example, after you've read the chapter on resilience, you'll be able to read the "Yes Brain Kids" section with your child and discuss together what it means to face fears and overcome obstacles, and how to do so in daily life.

The second section at the close of each chapter is called "My Own Yes Brain." Here we'll give you a chance to think about the ideas in that chapter not only as a parent who's looking to understand and give your child important skills, but also as an *individual* who's interested in lifelong growth and development yourself. After all, you're modeling for your child how to be in the world. As we always tell our audiences, virtually all of the ideas and techniques we teach will apply to adults as well as children. That doesn't mean you have to be perfect all the time or on top of things at every moment. But developing better communication and relational skills, being more open and receptive to new experiences, finding more meaning in everyday life, feeling happier and more fulfilled—who doesn't want that? And that's what the Yes Brain is all about. So each chapter will conclude by giving you a chance to think about your own life and how you might benefit from living in a way that's even more resilient, balanced, insightful, and empathic.

At the back of the book you'll find the "Yes Brain Refrigerator Sheet," where we very briefly summarize the main ideas of the book. You can copy this sheet and put it on your fridge, or snap a photo with your phone and refer to it when you want to recall key ideas or tell others about the Yes Brain.

Everything we present in these pages is backed by science. But we realize as well that parents are, pretty much by definition, overwhelmed and exhausted, frequently struggling just to find a few minutes here and there to eat and sleep and go to the bathroom. So we've worked hard to make things as simple and user-friendly as we could, keeping true to the science but joining with you as fellow parents to make things straightforward, accurate, and effective.

We're immensely honored that you've chosen to include us on this difficult and rewarding journey called parenting. In fact, we feel great respect and admiration that, with everything you have going on as you raise your children, you're still working hard to do so in an intentional, loving way instead of just switching on the autopilot and doing whatever you saw your parents do. That kind of loving intentionality will go a long way toward introducing your children to the Yes Brain and helping them approach the world with openness, excitement, and joy.

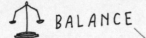

BALANCE

CHAPTER 2

The Balanced Yes Brain

lex loved watching his young son, Teddy, play soccer—as long as things were going well. If Teddy's team was winning, and if he was scoring goals, everything was great. But when he missed a shot or made a bad pass, or if his team lost, Teddy lost control. He immediately flipped his lid, losing the integrative role of his upstairs PFC, and now his downstairs brain began to take over. The same happened when it was his turn to sit out so other children could play. He would keep running back onto the field, and Alex sometimes had to hold him to keep him on the sidelines!

Teddy's reactions to disappointment were at least somewhat understandable—he was only eight, after all, and very competitive. And eight-year-olds sometimes have hard days where they don't handle themselves well. The problem was that his outbursts occurred so frequently, and over situations that didn't seem to ruffle the other eight-year-olds. In fact, Alex felt immediate dread when anything went south in one of Teddy's games. (And if you've watched eight-year-olds play soccer, you know that Alex had numerous occasions to feel that dread!) He knew that as soon as the team fell behind, or Teddy missed a slide tackle, or the referee made a call against him or the team, Teddy would begin to pout, cry, and sometimes stomp off the field and refuse to play.

What was Teddy needing at this moment of his life? Balance, the first fundamental that emerges from the Yes Brain. His ability to regulate himself—which means balancing his emotions and body—was lacking, so it didn't take much to dysregulate him and send him out of control.

We're guessing you experience something like this with your own kids from time to time, where they become dysregulated and have difficulty controlling their emotions and behaviors. Maybe you've seen your kids act like Teddy when they don't get their way. Or they might have their own unique way of letting you know when they're not able to control themselves. Younger children, when they're out of balance, will tantrum or throw things, or hit or kick or bite. Some of these same actions show up in older kids who are dysregulated, but they'll also learn to push their parents' buttons, using their developing vocabulary and understanding of psychology to wound their parents with what they say. Other kids, both younger and older, will just shut down or hide, either literally or figuratively, blocking everyone else out and suffering alone.

The point is that all kids lose their emotional balance. It might happen more or less frequently, but becoming dysregulated is simply par for the childhood course. In fact, if it seems like your child *never* becomes upset or loses control, then that's probably cause for concern. Some kids rigidly control their emotions so that they never get overwhelmed, and if they go too far in this direction they risk emotionally blocking a sense of vitality that comes from a balanced emotional life. Childhood is about learning to experience a wide array of types and intensities of emotion, and that, by necessity, means sometimes "losing control" as the intensity of emotions overwhelms the ability to think clearly. Welcome to being human!

A lack of balance and frequent reactivity can stem from all kinds of sources:

- Developmental age
- Temperament
- Trauma
- Sleep problems
- Sensory processing challenges
- Health and medical issues
- Learning, cognitive, and other disabilities and discrepancies
- Caregivers who amplify distress or who are unresponsive
- Mismatch of environmental demands and child's capacity
- Mental health disorders

These causes of reactivity affect kids to varying degrees, but the results, again, are recognizable: emotional chaos in the form of explosive anger—yelling, acting out, disrespectful outbursts, intense anxiety—and/or withdrawal or rigidity in the form of shutting down, depression, and self-isolation. Notice how these sets of unbalanced responses are like two banks on either side of the central flow of a river of integrative balance: one bank is chaos, the other bank is rigidity. Balance is learning to flow down that central stream of being flexible, adaptive, coherent (resilient over time), energized, and stable—the FACES flow of balance that comes with integration.

There's a reason that balance is the first of the four Yes Brain fundamentals. In a very real sense, the other three fundamentals—resilience, insight, and empathy—all depend on a child's being able to exhibit a certain amount of emotional balance and control. In fact, all the lessons we want to teach our kids, along with all the outcomes we'd like to see—meaningful relationships with family and friends, restorative sleep, success in school, a general sense of happiness in life—depend on balance. Plus, when kids are out of control, they can't learn. It makes no sense to try to teach a lesson to a child who's in the middle of a tantrum. She can hardly even hear you, much less follow directions or make good decisions about how to respond to her feelings.

All the lessons we want to teach our kids, along with all the outcomes we'd like to see—meaningful relationships with family and friends, effective sleep, success in school, a general sense of happiness in life—depend on balance. So one of our primary jobs as parents, regardless of the age of our children, is to help them be more balanced.

To put it as simply as possible, balance is crucial for every aspect of your child's functioning. When a child is out of balance and out of control, whatever the cause, the reactive behavior can make things stressful and difficult for everyone—especially the child himself. So one of our primary jobs as parents, regardless of the age of our children, is to help them be more balanced by "co-regulating." That means supporting them as they regain emotional composure, as well as teaching them skills that will help them stay balanced and regulated more easily in the future. Let's talk about how you can do just that.

Balance Is a Skill to Be Learned

Despite his out-of-control behavior on the soccer field, Teddy didn't necessarily have a mood or behavioral disorder that required a long-term therapeutic intervention or a medication evaluation. And he definitely didn't need a No Brain response from his father, where Alex punished him or shamed him for losing control. Instead, Teddy needed his dad to offer a Yes Brain response focused on helping him achieve emotional balance by developing new skills to regulate himself.

This is what Tina explained to Alex when he visited her office. For some children, professional intervention is needed and very helpful in expanding their "window of tolerance" and improving their ability to regulate their brains and bodies. "Window of tolerance" is a term Dan coined to mean the width of a span of activation in the brain within which we can function well. Beyond the upper edge of the window our mind becomes chaotic; beyond the lower edge we become rigid. When the window for a given emotion, like sadness or anger, is quite narrow, it's easy in that emotional state to "lose it" with a small provocation. With another emotion, such as fear, the same child may be able to tolerate a wide amount before she becomes chaotic or rigid.

There are many issues that can make a given child's window quite narrow. For example, behavior like Teddy's *can* be indicative of a sensory processing disorder, ADHD, a history of trauma, or something else that could narrow his window for frustration. In this case, he might benefit from assessment and intervention. But as Tina explained to Alex, Teddy primarily needed to develop self-regulation skills. His behavior, like all behavior, was actually a form of communication, and it was screaming—to his father and everyone else within shouting distance of the soccer field—that he didn't yet have the skills or strategies needed to feel balanced and in control of his own emotions and actions. Tina worked with Alex, and with Teddy, on developing some of these regulation skills to help expand his windows of tolerance (as we'll explain below).

Behavior is actually a form of communication.

That's really what a balanced brain means: the ability to achieve emotional stability and regulate the body and brain. It means considering our options and making good decisions—being flexible. And it means being able to return fairly quickly to stability after difficult moments and feelings, the basis of equanimity. It means maintaining control of one's mind and emotions and behaviors and handling difficult emotions and circumstances well. When we occasionally burst out of the window of tolerance, as life can have us do, we will eventually come back to emotional equilibrium. All of this is what we mean by balance.

Another way to put it is that children with a balanced brain demonstrate *response flexibility*. Before immediately flying off the handle when something happens that they don't like, they adapt. They can pause and think about how best to respond to the situation. As opposed to a rigid, almost involuntary reaction to the circumstances, the child can realize that there are choices to be made and can make a good decision with a certain amount of flexibility (depending on the child's age and stage of development, of course). There's nothing at all wrong with Teddy's experiencing frustration, anger, and disappointment. In fact, it's good and healthy to feel these emotions. Remember, a meaningful life is an emotional life. Yet he needs to develop the skills to respond in a productive, healthy way while also feeling his emotions. And a balanced brain is able to feel the feelings, appropriately express them, and then flexibly recover and not allow them to take over and call the shots.

When children are very young, they don't yet have enough brain development to be able to consistently maintain emotional balance. (There's a reason someone coined the phrase "the terrible twos"— along with "the trying threes" and the "frustrating fours.") And because the upstairs brain is not fully developed yet, one of our jobs as caregivers is to use our own developed brains to help children regain balance. That's where co-regulation comes in. We help calm them down by being a soothing presence, which assures them they will be safe and that we will be with them during these big feelings that are overwhelming them.

We'll say much more about this idea below and in Chapter 3, but really, the key to helping your kids when they're out of control is to provide this loving, soothing presence. Most of the time, kids misbehave because they *can't* control their emotions and bodies right then, not because they *won't*. So before you ever begin to teach them lessons or talk to them about what you want from them or what they should or should not do, they need you to help them regain balance. You do this through connection—by holding them, soothing them, listening to them, empathizing with them, and helping them feel safe and loved. This is how balance returns. Then, and only then, does it make sense to talk to them about appropriate behavior or handling themselves better in the future.

Keep in mind that kids don't like feeling out of control. When they're dysregulated, it's scary for them. We can help them regain their emotional balance. When they don't have our help, they may be left to deal with the intense and stressful emotional dysregulation on their own. That's when we'll often see the dreaded tantrum: *The tail broke off my goldfish cracker, and it's the worst thing that's ever happened to me! Put it back on! Put it back on!* This kind of reactive, intense response is developmentally appropriate at a certain age. But as children grow and development unfolds, we can make it safe for them to experience a wide range of emotions, even intense ones, and then help them flexibly return to balance, so they can enjoy the benefits of a Yes Brain.

> Most of the time, kids misbehave because they *can't* control their emotions and bodies right then, not because they *won't*. So before you ever begin to teach them lessons or talk to them about what you want from them, they need you to help them regain balance.

Balance and the Green Zone

Here's a helpful way to think about the window of tolerance. You might remember learning, in your science classes a long time ago, about your autonomic nervous system. There are two branches of your nervous system that are more evolved—the sympathetic nervous system (which works like the gas pedal to rev us up and amplify our emotional and physical arousal, such as increasing our heart rate and pace of breathing and increasing muscle tone that allows us to get up and move) and the parasympathetic nervous system (which works more like the brakes to calm us down and lower our nervous system arousal, where we breathe more slowly and our muscles relax). When we are in a safe environment, these two branches are fluidly interacting in ways that explain a lot about our various states throughout the day. When you get sleepy in that afternoon meeting, you have more parasympathetic activity, and when you get frustrated and tense as you sit in traffic on the way home, or when you're upset with your kids, you have more sympathetic arousal. The researcher Stephen Porges has developed what he calls the Polyvagal Theory to explain how the arousal of our nervous system impacts our bodies and social engagement systems.

Here's a simple model that explains the idea visually. Many different experts have used multiple variations of this type of model, which in its simplest form focuses on three zones your child may experience at a given moment.

When the two branches of the nervous system are well balanced, we handle ourselves well. We can call this state the "green zone," and it signifies that a person is in a Yes Brain state. This is when you are inside the window of tolerance. When a child is in the green zone, his body, emotions, and behavior are regulated. He is in balance, and his sympathetic accelerator and parasympathetic brakes are working in a coordinated way. He feels in control and handles himself well, even if he's facing adversity or experiencing negative emotions such as frustration, sadness, fear, anger, or anxiety. (See the image below. This book is in black and white, but you get the idea.)

RED ZONE

GREEN ZONE

BLUE ZONE

At times, though, things don't go his way and his emotions overwhelm him. This means that the intensity of the emotion has burst past the window of tolerance's boundaries. For a younger child it might be that she can't have a second ice pop, or his friends exclude him on the playground, or she feels really frustrated that she keeps crashing when learning how to ride a bike. For an older child it might have to do with pitching a bad game, or getting a bad grade, or being angered by a sibling. As will happen in the life of every individual, she doesn't get what she wants, or she feels intense fear, panic, anger, frustration, or embarrassment. Put most simply, she can't handle the demands of the situation. And all of a sudden, it becomes much harder to maintain balance and remain in the calm, contented green zone.

So instead, the child enters the "red zone." This is what consistently happened to Teddy, who was a frequent flyer in the red zone. Alex could see the obvious physical red-zone signals that appeared when Teddy's gas pedal was floored. His heart rate and breathing rapidly increased. His eyes would narrow or get really wide. He would clench his teeth, make fists, and tense his muscles. His body temperature would rise and his skin would become red or splotchy. The more scientific way to describe this red-zone state is that the child's autonomic nervous system goes into a state of *hyperarousal*, activating an acute stress response. His downstairs brain takes over control of his emotions and body and, therefore, his behavior. The result might be a tantrum, or lashing out at those around him, or throwing objects, or a combination of all of this and more. Typical red-zone behaviors can also be yelling, biting, physical or verbal aggression, shaking, crying, laughing inappropriately, and more. If you're like most parents, right now you can picture your own child and what it looks like as he or she enters the red zone.

This red-zone blowup is what happens when we lose control. It's a No Brain state that explains what's going on when kids (and sometimes adults, who might fittingly describe the experience as "seeing red") act in ways we typically would not. In fact, a lot of behavioral problems, which kids may be punished for, are actually red-zone symptoms, where kids aren't fully *choosing* to behave the way they are; they've just lost control and often *can't* make good choices or "stop crying" or "calm down right this instant." Those are No Brain responses.

Instead, Alex and Tina came up with a four-pronged Yes Brain response to Teddy's situation. First, they taught Teddy himself about the red zone. Second, they taught him calming techniques, such as slowing his breathing. Third, they gave him practice dealing with tolerable frustration with lots of role-play and board games where things didn't always go his way, but in the context of a low-stakes game. Small frustrations prepared him to better handle big ones, such as losing a soccer game. This is how they were teaching him to widen his window of tolerance for frustration. Finally, Tina worked with Alex on first soothing and comforting Teddy when he became upset, and addressing the behavior later once Teddy could be calm and actually hear what his dad was telling him. (By the way, we'll discuss each of these strategies in detail at different parts of the book.)

Sometimes, though, kids get upset and *don't* enter the red zone. At times a lack of balance sends them into the "blue zone." Here the defense strategies are less about red-zone fight-and-flight and more about an immobilizing freeze-or-faint response. In the blue zone, a child responds to a negative situation not by acting out but by shutting down. This response occurs in varying degrees. Some kids might simply emotionally withdraw, becoming quiet and leaving everyone else on the outside, unable to help. Others might actually physically remove themselves from the situation. Some go into an extreme state called dissociation, an internal disconnection of their feelings from thoughts and even bodily sensations. Dissociation is even more likely to occur if there's a history of trauma.

The physical signs of a blue-zone faint or collapse response are a lower heart rate and blood pressure, slower breathing, floppy muscles and posture, and a lack of eye contact. This can look similar to how an opossum plays dead to ward off danger. We can also sometimes see an immobilized freeze response, where the muscles tighten,

A No Brain response further frustrates a child

A Yes Brain response calms a child and helps build skills

heart rate speeds up, and there is a temporary lack of movement, a stilling, that is an activated state but without motion. The blue-zone response turns inward, rather than exploding outward. Whereas the red zone represents *hyper*arousal in the autonomic nervous system, the blue zone can be seen as a kind of *hypo*arousal, which engages the brake pedal in distinct ways: the faint response shuts down internal physiology, and the freeze turns down outward movement. Children enter the blue zone when they see no clear escape from a situation that seems uncomfortable, scary, or dangerous.

Rarely is a "choice" made about which state to be in. The nervous system automatically determines which response seems most adaptive for the situation based on many factors, including current circumstances, memory of past experiences, and innate temperament.

There are many ways people respond to difficult situations and intense emotions, and we're very much simplifying here to explain our point. The main idea, though, is that kids in the green zone generally handle themselves well, making good decisions and maintaining balance and control over their emotions, bodies, and decisions. They remain open to engaging with the world around them in healthy and meaningful ways, and are most receptive to learning. This is how they are working within their window, the green zone. Then when they get overwhelmed by emotion or threat in their environment, they become reactive, entering either the chaotic, explosive red zone or the shut-down, rigid, and unresponsive blue zone. Either way, they are unable to be balanced and handle themselves well, whereas kids in the flexible green zone can find new and productive ways to respond to challenging moments. That's when they are working within their window of tolerance. All kids will enter the red or blue zone at some point; it's what children (and adults) do, and we should encourage them to experience the full range of their emotions. But kids who have a hardy, wide green zone as an inner resource can experience frustration, disappointment, sadness, and fear, all while still remaining in their green zone. Here they have a wide set of windows of tolerance for a broad spectrum of emotional experiences, even the intense ones. They are balanced and adaptable even in the face of challenge and adversity.

All of this leads to a pretty obvious conclusion for parents: if we want to help our kids become more balanced, so they can remain regulated and handle life's difficulties with more grace and composure, we have two main jobs: to help them get back into the green zone when they become upset, and to help them expand their green zone over time. That's how we give them the gift of a wide set of windows within which they can experience the world.

Chapter 3 will discuss how to expand and build your child's green zone. But here, let's focus on what you can do to help your kids to get back into and remain in their green zone.

> If we want to help our kids become more balanced, so they can remain regulated and handle life's difficulties with more grace and composure, we need to help them get back into the green zone when they become upset, and help them expand their green zone over time.

How Balanced Is Your Child?

Think about your own child in terms of emotional flexibility and behavioral balance. Ask yourself some questions regarding how hardy your child's green zone is, how challenging circumstances and big feelings typically affect your child, and which emotions have more narrow windows and which have wider ones.

As we've said, it's natural for kids to lose their emotional balance at various times. It's important, then, for parents to think about what triggers No Brain reactivity in each child, and how to help him return to balance once his regulation goes off-kilter and results in big, chaotic, red-zone reactions or collapsed, rigid, blue-zone responses. Based on Bruce McEwen's work regarding toxic stress, we've developed questions we've been using in our offices for years to help parents investigate how they can support their kids when they're struggling. Think about your individual kids, and ask yourself a few questions:

- *How wide is my child's green zone for particular emotions?*
  In other words, how easily does she handle discomfort, fear, anger, and disappointment? Considering her age and developmental stage, is she able to deal with setbacks without quickly veering into the red or blue zones?
- *How easily does my child leave the green zone?* What kind of emotion or situation does it take to send him into the

chaotic red or rigid blue? Keeping in mind, again, his age and developmental stage, do minor issues set him off, sending him outside the green zone and into emotional dysregulation?

- *Are there typical triggers that lead my child to imbalance?* Do the triggers have to do with physical needs like being hungry or tired? Are there certain emotional or social skills that are lacking and need to be practiced?

- *How far outside the green zone does my child go?* When she enters the red or blue zone, how intense is the reaction? How imbalanced does her chaos or rigidity become once she's outside the green zone?

- *How long does my child stay outside the green zone, and how easily does he return?* How resilient is your child? Once he becomes dysregulated, how hard is it for him to regain a sense of balance and self-control?

We'll be exploring these issues and ideas for the remainder of the chapter (and the book), so the more accurately you can assess your own child's unique skills and temperament, the better you'll be at applying the strategies we discuss. Everything we talk about here aims at helping your kids achieve more balance in the short term—making everyday life easier and more peaceful—while also helping you teach them lifelong skills so they can spend more time in the green zone and grow into teenagers and adults who handle themselves well and live with peace and equanimity.

Dan helped a young mom experience these short- and long-term benefits of the Yes Brain when she came to him because even after weeks of a slow, thoughtful adjustment period, her kindergartner was regularly falling apart whenever he had to be away from her. While the other children had gotten used to saying goodbye to their parents, his intense separation anxiety caused major problems at school drop-off. He would promise that he'd go to school, and he and his mom would make detailed proactive plans, but at eight o'clock each morning he'd enter the red zone. At the carpool circle he'd begin to yell, spit, bite, and even rip his clothes.

This caring, worried mother came to Dan for help. When it came to separating from her, her son's green zone was tiny, almost nonexistent. He lost balance quickly because of this one particular trigger, and he went far into the red zone, unable to return to balance until his mom promised not to leave.

Dan's approach with this mom was to teach her essentially what we'll explain for the rest of this chapter. He began by helping her understand that her presence was her son's best strategy for staying regulated. The problem was that when she left, he didn't have other effective strategies to keep himself in the green zone. His connection to his mother kept him regulated. At times she resented how oppressive his need could feel, but Dan explained to her that her son's need to be with her was his best adaptive, coping strategy to help deal with his fear and anxiety. Similar to a baby crying or a toddler running to her dad when she heard a scary noise, her son was relying on her to help him tolerate the stress of the situation and deal with his inner chaos and imbalance. This coping strategy made sense, but because he didn't have other skills and strategies to help him regulate his emotions and tolerate the separation, it was causing distress for both him and his mom.

A No Brain response would have based "success" on whether the boy was compliant, regardless of how much distress he experienced. It might have relied on shame ("None of the *other* kids need their mommies here") or minimizing the boy's feelings ("You're a big boy;

there's no need to be sad"). Dan, instead, helped the mother offer a Yes Brain approach that acknowledged, honored, and responded to her son's emotions. First the mom and her son wrote and illustrated a book together about how hard it is to say goodbye in the morning, but about how fun school is once he gets there. Then they practiced separations for very short periods in locations where he felt comfortable and safe, gradually expanding the time and making the separation more tolerable. They also talked about "brave body" posture and

A No Brain response increases the feelings of distress

A Yes Brain response focuses on his feelings and builds skills

how it feels different from "worry body" posture, and they practiced the "brave body" version. Finally they asked for help from his teacher, who offered to meet them at the drop-off circle and allow his mom to stay with him at first. Then gradually (as quickly as he could tolerate) she moved farther away and was gone for longer periods of time, thus progressively widening his window of tolerance for separation. With these steps the mother was able to acknowledge and respect her son's experience and emotions.

These techniques proved to be successful with this child, but every child is different. The point isn't to memorize a set of steps, but to help kids build skills and create space and opportunities to encourage a more balanced brain. The foundation for helping your children be more balanced (and resilient and kind and ethical) is your connection with them. It all, and always, begins with relationship.

Integration in the Parent-Child Relationship

Earlier we talked about how integration within an individual brain leads to a Yes Brain. We said that integration occurs when different parts of the brain do their respective jobs, while also teaming up to accomplish important tasks more effectively than they could on their own. The same concept applies in the relationship between a parent and a child.

Integration works when *differentiated* parts are also *linked*. For example, in an interpersonal relationship, each person maintains his or her own individuality while working together as a coordinated whole. Integration in this way is not the same as blending or making all the same and homogenous. Integration has the essential feature of retaining the differences and establishing connections that don't obliterate those differences. That's one reason healthy, integrated relationships can be so challenging—we need to be both different and linked.

This is especially important in the parent-child relationship, where there are two individuals who are closely connected, but where we also honor differences, thereby promoting healthy integration. Ideally, here's how it looks: A child gets upset. Maybe your three-year-old becomes furious because you tell her she can't watch her TV show because she's already had her allotted screen time for the day. As she moves into the red zone and begins to tantrum, you immediately empathically connect with her, so that she feels understood and listened to. Using an empathic tone of voice and a soft facial expression, your words might sound like this: "You really wanted to watch another one. Are you feeling mad and sad? Yes, that's hard. I get it. I'm right here."

You don't change your mind about the show, but she knows you're listening and that you're there for her. That's the *linked* part of integration. Linking brain to brain, you're deeply attuned to your child's emotional state and offer a contingent response when she goes off-kilter and begins to melt down. "Contingent" means your communication to her directly responds in a positive way to what she's communicating to you. As a result of this attuned linkage—where you tune in to her internal state, not just her outward behavior—you can notice and help her when she moves toward the red zone or the blue zone and collapses into hopeless and helpless places. Instead of just reacting to the external actions, you are focusing your attention on what her inner world may be like—red, green, or blue—and communicating to that internal state of your child. You are also giving her the support and practice to tolerate difficult feelings, and showing her that you can handle her emotions, even when she can't. She can learn to widen her window of tolerance through your attuned communication with her.

We've discussed this idea in detail in other places, especially in our book *No-Drama Discipline*. As we explain there, discipline is about teaching and building skills so that over time, you need to discipline less because your kids are building skills to become more *self-*disciplined. And since the essence of discipline is to teach, kids have to be in a state of mind that allows them to learn. That's right—the green zone. Typically, the most effective way to help a child who is upset and reactive move back into the green zone is connection. All kids are different, and we always want to be mindful of developmental and individual differences. But for the most part, and in most cases, when a child is out of balance and losing control, the most effective parental response (for everyone's sanity and even for effective discipline) is to connect and redirect.

This strategy requires that we connect first—before trying to teach a lesson or address behavior or problem-solve. Just as we would if our child were physically hurt, we want to comfort our child when she is hurting emotionally. Connecting means offering empathy and a soothing presence through physical affection, empathic facial expressions, and loving, understanding words. It works even more effectively if we can sit in a relaxed posture that is *below* our child's eye level and if we say empathically, "I'm right here with you." This type of connection helps the child move back into the green zone, where she becomes calmer and more receptive to what we have to say. Then we can redirect toward better behavior and decision-making, and talk about other strategies to try next time a similar situation comes up. This is where we set limits that help our children feel safe and hold them accountable for their behavior, including making things right and engaging in appropriate repairs. That's the connect-and-redirect approach in a nutshell, and it relies heavily on our being linked to our child and attuned to his or her feelings.

But a healthy, Yes Brain parental response leaves room for *differentiation* as well. In other words, you don't want to lose differentiation and tip the balance so that instead of having both differences and connection, you and your child become *overly* linked. This lack of balance in the relationship, meaning connecting with your child without maintaining a differentiated you, can lead to difficulty with balance within your child. It's important to emphasize here that the balance of integration doesn't mean you should keep your distance or stop loving your child. It simply means that both linkage and differentiation are what we can encourage as fundamental parts of love and support. This is an important distinction, so let's look closely at an example.

When a child shuts down or veers into volatility, your job isn't to take on her emotions yourself, or to rescue her completely from them, or to prevent her from ever dealing with anything difficult. Rather than running for the superglue to reattach the tail of the goldfish cracker or dashing out to the store to buy a new box, you remain linked and attuned, but differentiated as well: *I know, love. You're really mad, aren't you, about the goldfish breaking? It's disappointing right now.*

As a result, even though you don't "fix" her problem in the moment, she experiences your empathy and connection at a deep level, which allows her to move back into a state of balance and regulation. She'll actually feel safer in life experiencing that differentiation and knowing that you can contain her dysregulation without becoming out of control yourself. You and your well-functioning upstairs brain help bring her upstairs brain back online so she can move back into the green zone. In this type of co-regulation, you are letting her feel her feelings while you provide a safety net, a "soft place to fall," so she isn't left alone in her distress.

Imagine if you were to lose your own integrated state to match her state of dysregulation. That would be losing differentiation and having excess linkage. In that case, if she were crying, you would fall down on the floor and start sobbing, too. Lots of mirroring, no differentiation. Instead, you walk with her through her frustration and emotional chaos without immediately rescuing her from it, and then you help guide her back into green-zone balance through your presence, touch, and empathy. The differentiation in the relationship means that you allow her to experience the inevitable difficult emotions of life, but the linkage means that you stay connected enough to keep her safe and help her regain balance. That's the power of integration to cultivate well-being in our lives. And that's the art of Yes Brain parenting.

Again, that's the Yes Brain ideal: to be differentiated enough to allow children to face difficult experiences and feel their feelings, while remaining linked enough that you can provide boundaries and comfort to quickly help them move back into the green zone, and even expand it for the future. It's what we call the Yes Brain sweet spot.

The Yes Brain Sweet Spot: Are You Maintaining a Strong Balance?

Ideally, since all of our reactions and responses to our kids build or diminish their Yes Brain growth, we would most often hit the sweet

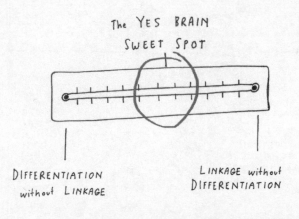

spot and offer just enough linkage, and just enough differentiation. No parenting is ideal, though. None of us provide optimal parenting all the time. Often we respond in a way that doesn't integrate the two.

Emotionally dismissive parenting leads to

Minimizing

Criticizing/Shaming

Distancing

On one extreme of the integration spectrum are the parents who are so differentiated that they become distant from their child. They are dismissive of their kids' emotions and respond to emotional imbalance by minimizing or criticizing their children for their feelings. As a result, their children may be left to deal with problems on their own, even problems that they're not developmentally ready to address.

We often fail to realize the harm we're doing when we condemn and disparage our kids and their feelings. When we distract, deny, or degrade; when we blame or deliver a bootstrap lecture; when we remove ourselves or shut them down and embarrass them for their feelings—when we respond to their emotions with any of these responses, we effectively punish them for feeling healthy, human sentiments and for expressing what's going on inside. This can lead to the numbing of all emotions, teaching kids that feelings and experiences should not be shared.

Rather than being helped to return to the green zone, and instead of building skills they can use in the future when they experience big feelings, they remain in a dysregulated state without any support. So they're left with two options: either become more upset and leave the green zone, or learn to hide their true feelings from us. Differentiation without enough linkage leaves children to weather emotional storms without any help. No wonder they can't achieve emotional and behavioral balance.

The other extreme of the integration spectrum is problematic in a different way, and it occurs when parents become only *linked* and there's not enough differentiation. We sometimes call this enmeshment. It occurs when a parent fails to honor a child's individuality, or when the mom's or dad's identity becomes *exclusively* "parent." It produces the phenomenon that has come to be known as "helicopter parenting," and it leads to the mother who is devastated and personally wounded because her four-year-old is going through a phase where he only wants his dad to put him to bed at night. Or to the father who does his middle-schooler's homework or, while working in his daughter's preschool class one day, is unable to follow the teacher's admonition to let his daughter struggle at peeling her own banana.

Sometimes we're so linked that we don't provide enough differentiation

These are examples where parents need to be less linked and more differentiated—for the sake of their kids, and for their own sake as well. These parents display discomfort when their kids experience a range of emotions and desires and individuality. They have such a

narrow window of tolerance for their children's unhappiness or struggle that they repeatedly act on their behalf and rescue them, rather than letting them feel, try, make mistakes, and learn.

We can all get a bit too involved in our kids' lives from time to time. It's a real temptation that emerges out of our love for them. Sometimes we're doing more than we should. We tie their shoes, or we walk to the counter to ask for extra ketchup, instead of letting our kids accomplish these tasks for themselves. Or sometimes they're facing some difficulty or challenge, and we jump in right away to rescue them, to stand up for them, to "make things right." We talk to a teacher. We address conflict with their friend. We call their coach.

Of course there are times we need to stand up for and defend our children. At times we need to be absolutely fierce in doing so. So let's make sure we're clear here: nothing is more important than your relationship with your child. If you've read anything either of us has written over the years, you know how much we emphasize child-parent attachment. Put simply, it's impossible to "spoil" your kids by giving them too much love or attention. You don't need to worry that you're a helicopter parent because you're providing lots of love and affection. In fact, more and more research shows that as parents have become more invested in their kids' welfare and development over the last few decades, children have become healthier and happier and safer. They stay out of trouble more, stay in school longer, and do better academically. According to almost any metric, children do better when their parents emphasize attunement and connection in the relationship.

That being said, though, part of loving our kids means avoiding the extreme, linkage-without-differentiation end of the integration spectrum, where we step in and handle their problems, short-circuiting their opportunity to learn how to address difficult issues. Having to self-advocate with a teacher or address a problem with a friend can be a powerful learning opportunity. So we want to give our kids the benefit of getting practice using their problem-solving upstairs brain, along with their voice and their communication skills.

Plus, in letting them handle situations themselves, we teach them that they can tolerate discomfort. A great way to build resilience and confidence is to have to deal with a challenging situation and come out successful on the other side. When they undergo repeated experiences where they assess a situation, wrestle with the problem, then come up with possible solutions, their brains become wired to be more adept at doing so in the future.

We want to teach children to assert themselves, and to understand that we believe in them and their ability to handle situations on their own. They can then discover how strong and capable they really are, even if they don't know it. They can walk away from a difficult experience with an "I did it!"

Another way to say it is that we want to avoid bubble-wrapping our kids. Our kids are precious, but they're not fragile.

When we bubble-wrap our children and protect them from any discomfort, distress, or potential challenge, we actually make them *more* fragile, leaving them less capable of achieving balance on their own. We explicitly and inadvertently communicate to them, "I don't think you can handle this, and you need me to shelter you or do it for you." In so doing, we deny them the privilege of the practice of feeling, sitting in discomfort, and persevering, then finding their way out and seeing that they are strong and resourceful.

Want your children to believe that you believe in them? Want them to be resourceful and resilient and emotionally balanced? Want them to be able to develop grit and a sturdy, robust bandwidth for tolerating challenges, which they can then rise to meet? Want them to know that they are not victims to their emotions and their circumstances? Then let them feel. Let them wrestle with indecision, discomfort, discouragement, and disappointment.

Avoid, in other words, becoming so linked to your children that there's no room for differentiation. Remember, our job as parents is not to rescue our kids from hard things and uncomfortable feelings. Our job is to walk with them through their difficult moments with connection and empathy, allowing them to feel, to be active participants in problem-solving, and to discover the depth of their own capacity. It's out of our deep love for our children that we want to protect them, but their capacity will be greater if we allow that love to lead us to our own courage, so that we can feel strong enough to let them discover their own strength.

> Our job is to walk with our children through their difficult moments with connection and empathy, allowing them to feel, to be active participants in problem-solving, and to discover the depth of their own capacity. It's out of our deep love for our children that we want to protect them, but their capacity will be greater if we allow that love to lead us to our own courage, so that we can feel strong enough to let them discover their own strength.

Your job is to be there, ready to help and comfort when they fall, while letting them acquire the important lessons that come with learning to balance. You want to find that Yes Brain sweet spot, with a healthy and appropriate amount of both differentiation and linkage.

Balanced Schedule, Balanced Brain

Most of what we've said so far is about helping kids achieve *internal* balance so they can regulate their brains and bodies. One important *external* factor that contributes to emotional regulation is how much space you create in your child's life to allow for healthy growth and development. In other words, there's a clear link between a balanced brain and a balanced schedule, where kids are allowed to be kids without having every second planned and every moment gobbled up by homework and programmed activities.

To a large extent, children develop emotional regulation skills through friendships, spontaneous play, and free time, where they are afforded the opportunity to be curious and imaginative. A less-

Avoid the extremes of the Integration Spectrum
Not enough linkage

Not enough differentiation

scheduled calendar also allows for more time with family and friends to learn all the lessons that come with those relationships. Even boredom creates important openings for growth and learning. We worry so much about our kids' academic lives, but one of the most valuable educational things you can offer a child when you hear the ubiquitous summertime complaint "I'm bored" is to respond with some version of "See what you can think of to do in the yard. I see a shovel, some duct tape, and a torn-up garden hose. Have a blast!"

We heard a terrifically illustrative story about Richard Feynman, the Nobel Prize–winning physicist, from a friend who had met him when she was about fourteen years old. Given the chance to pick his brain, she asked him how he got so smart. He said it was simple. From age four, his parents essentially locked him out of the house, behind which was a junkyard. The young Feynman would tinker with abandoned machines and motors, and eventually began to fix clocks. Simple boredom and the need to find something to do led to all kinds of mental challenges and intellectual growth, which eventually created one of the finest minds of the last several decades. And while we're not advocating locking kids out of the house or giving them free rein in a junkyard, and we're not promising that doing so will lead to a Nobel Prize, we do encourage parents to give their kids enough space and free time to discover the world and who they are.

This fits in with what leaders at NASA and the Jet Propulsion Laboratory say about needing to alter their recruiting process. Previously, emphasis was on hiring the graduates with the best grades from the "best" schools in the country, but they began to notice that many of these young adults weren't necessarily very good at solving problems. They had learned to master the academic system, and they had earned plenty of academic gold stars. But their emphasis on "coloring within the lines" and operating well in a No Brain culture didn't inevitably translate into discovering creative and unique approaches to solving difficult dilemmas. So in their recruitment process these agencies began to prioritize finding grads with a strong history of playing or working with their hands throughout childhood and adolescence. It was people who had built things as kids, with a strong history of play, who were the best problem-solvers.

All of this highlights that aside from prizing and prioritizing your relationship with your kids, the other main way you can help create balance in their lives is by protecting their time and maintaining plenty of opportunity for good old child-directed free play. Allow them time to explore and discover, and to develop important emotional, social, and intellectual skills through play and trial and error. When every second is scheduled, a child misses out on these opportunities.

The Science of Play

It's really not an exaggeration to say that free play is becoming an endangered activity for many of today's children. At home, play time is crowded out by structured activities, lessons, and practices. At school, academics start earlier and earlier, with more teaching (requiring more sitting) focused on increasing the child's ability to demonstrate mastery and perform well on standardized tests, leaving less and less time for children to build towers, play tag, and engage in pretend play. Plus, other contemporary social forces encroach on what was previously play's domain, as media, electronics, and the like assert their dominance in the lives and minds of kids.

None of these competing forces are inherently bad. But a real problem emerges when they more and more come to replace play, which is actually *essential* for optimal development in both humans and other mammals. Did you know, for instance, that even if the higher parts of a rat's brain, the upstairs cortex, are not functioning well, the rat will experience limitations to its cognitive abilities such as memory and learning, but it will continue to play? This finding by the neuroscientist Jaak Panksepp strongly suggests that the need for and drive to play are deep-seated, even primitive mammalian drives, and that they involve the downstairs, lower structures of the brain as do other instinctive urges for survival and connection. These lower regions directly influence the growth of higher cortical regions as well, enabling a more integrated brain to develop. Another study, this one by Stuart Brown that focused on murderers on death row, found two main commonalities in the murderers' various childhoods: they were abused in some way, and they were deprived of play as children.

Studies like these point out the importance not of dedicating childhood exclusively to hours of piano lessons, chemistry camp, and after-school academic programs, but instead of recognizing the fundamental need for kids to be allowed to be kids and just play. Music and science and academics are important, of course, and screen time has its place as well. Obviously, we're not against children's achieving mastery of skills. If there's a deep passion for a particular talent, that passion should be pursued. But not at the cost of giving children the chance to imagine and be curious and simply play, all of which will allow them to grow, develop, and discover who they are. Think about it this way: free play is a Yes Brain activity because the child is simply exploring her own imagination, trying out things in her behaviors and interactions with others, without judgment or threat. Free play is not the same as structured sports play. Both have their role in children's lives. With athletics, the rules and the common setup in which one team wins and another loses frequently set up a sense of evaluation of right and wrong. Having time for free play literally frees the child to explore her own imagination.

The drive to play is an ancient one that represents an inherent part of what humans are. Recent research demonstrates this point over and over again. Sometimes the studies show what we'd intuitively expect—that play reduces stress, for instance. We see this result, by the way, in high-resource and high-achieving communities and schools as well as in those that are impoverished and struggling. Other findings are a bit more surprising. For example, researchers have found that simply playing with toy blocks leads to increased language development in toddlers. Similarly, preschoolers who played after being dropped off at school were less distraught and tolerated the separation with more balance than their peers who were read to by their teachers. The simple act of playing serves as a protective factor when it comes to regulating emotions.

An unexamined perspective on play might assume that when children are playing they are just passing time or simply having fun—which is of course good—but that they are not exactly "accomplishing" anything or doing something "constructive" that would allow them to improve their minds. However, science-of-play studies demonstrate that the very act of playing offers countless benefits—both cognitive and non-cognitive—beyond just enjoying a moment (which, we strongly believe, is itself an inherently good thing to do). *Play is children's work.* It builds cognitive skills, improving language and problem-solving abilities as well as advancing other executive functions such as planning, predicting, anticipating consequences, and adjusting to surprises. Each of these is a Yes Brain skill! Play promotes integration. Children's social, relational, and even rhetorical skills improve when they play, as they have to negotiate playground politics and determine a game's or a group's explicit and implicit rules. They have to figure out how to enter play, negotiating with others when they don't get their way. They learn about fairness, about taking turns, about being flexible, about behaving ethically. And they're faced with dilemmas having to do with empathy as they determine how to respond to others who are left out.

Aside from these social benefits, play offers psychological and emotional advantages as well, helping create a balanced brain. When

they play, children get practice at developing all kinds of Yes Brain qualities, such as handling disappointment, sustaining attention, and making sense of their world. They try out roles and conquer fears and feelings of helplessness. They build emotional balance and resilience, and they develop the ability to tolerate frustration when they don't get their way. All because they are allowed to play.

Balance and the Overscheduled Child

When we talk to parents about play and the importance of free time and a balanced schedule, we inevitably get asked how we've handled the issue with our own kids. Before Tina had children, she decided that when she became a mom her kids would participate in only one activity at a time. She had heard about the dangers of the overscheduled child and how kids participating in too many activities would become tired and overwhelmed. They wouldn't have time to spend with their family, and they'd get burned out and begin to dislike whatever activity the parent was hoping they would embrace. All of this made sense to her, so she declared that if her kids wanted to take a dance class, that's all they'd do until the class was over. If they wanted to play a sport, they wouldn't be involved in anything else until the end of the season. She wasn't going to overschedule her children. (We're always ideal, excellent parents of hypothetical children!)

Then her first son came along, and she saw all the opportunities available to him, and all of his many different interests. She quickly came to see that her one-activity-at-a-time commitment was going to be tested. She and her husband wanted their son to learn piano. He also wanted to be involved in Cub Scouts with his friends from school. Plus it was immediately apparent that his passion was athletics. He wanted to play every sport in every season.

Piano. Scouts. Sports. Add in play dates, homework, and family outings, and how were they supposed to fit it all in? And he was just her first child. She now has three, all with their own opportunities and passions!

Dan experienced the same with his own kids, and spent many intense evenings and afternoons at various music performances and volleyball tournaments. It just goes with the parenting territory, and we're grateful that there are so many valuable and fun options available to our children. But how much is too much?

Once again, it comes down to balance and respecting individual differences. We do believe that overscheduling children is a legitimate concern in many homes. However, for some families, underscheduling, where kids are spending time in front of a screen for hours a day, is a problem. Our own respective kids have attended challenging schools and been involved in all kinds of activities, and at times we've worried that they're doing too much. But having spent many years trying to strike a healthy balance in terms of our kids' interests, we also want to be realistic and reasonable. Kids typically love to be active, and as long as it's healthy to do so and parents are making space for free time and not allowing the activity calendar to hold the whole family hostage, we want to feed their passions and let them participate in fun activities they love.

So how do we strike the healthy, Yes Brain balance? Here are some questions we encourage parents to ask themselves when they visit us in our offices:

- Does my child seem frequently tired or grumpy, or demonstrate other indicators of imbalance, such as showing signs of being under pressure or feeling anxious? Is my kid stressed out?
- Is my child so busy that he or she doesn't have unstructured time for playing and being creative?
- Is my child getting enough sleep? (If a child is involved in so many activities that he or she is just getting started on homework at bedtime, that's a problem.)

- Is my child's schedule so full that he or she doesn't have time to just hang out with friends or siblings?
- Are we all too busy to eat dinner together regularly? (You don't have to eat every meal together, but if you're rarely eating together, that's a concern.)
- Are you saying "hurry up" all the time to your children?
- Are you yourself so active and stressed that a majority of your interactions with your child are reactive and impatient?

Answering yes to any of these questions is an opportunity to pause and consider. If you said yes more than once, then we'd recommend that you give serious thought to whether your child is doing too much.

On the other hand, if none of the signs of overscheduling appear in your child, then you probably don't have to worry about this issue. Most likely your child is active, growing, and happy, and you've found a way to strike a healthy balance that both fosters Yes Brain growth and allows a Yes Brain to thrive. Keep in mind, too, that every child is different, and each will have a different drive and threshold for the rhythm of their days and weeks. It's important that we honor each child's uniqueness.

What You Can Do: Yes Brain Strategies That Promote Balance

Yes Brain Strategy #1 for Promoting a Balanced Brain: Maximize the ZZZ's

We are a nation of chronically sleep-deprived people. In young people, we continue to see far too much anxiety and depression, and many of the symptoms associated with these two diagnoses may result from or be amplified by chronic sleep deprivation. Children, especially, frequently have their sleep forfeited as a result of their parents' or school's well-meaning pursuit to maximally fill their days with enrichment activities. Ironically, parents are often so invested in making sure their children get time for fun and family, in addition to all the educational activities, that the all-important sleep is sacrificed on the enrichment altar, and bedtime gets pushed later and later into the evening.

The reduced amount of rest is a problem because sleep is essential for a balanced brain and body. New views of sleep, for example, suggest that adequate sleep is necessary to allow the inevitable toxins of the daytime's neural firing to be cleaned up so we can start the new day with a fresh, cleaned-up brain! Sleep is brain hygiene. Without enough, all sorts of brain and body processes are compromised, such as our ability to pay attention, remember, learn, be patient and flexible, and even properly process the food we eat.

A growing child obviously needs even more sleep than adults. The American Academy of Sleep Medicine, whose guidelines have been endorsed by the American Academy of Pediatrics, recommends the following for each respective age group:

HOW MUCH SLEEP DO KIDS NEED?

AGES		
4-12 mo. ⇨	12 - 16 hrs.	(including naps)
1 - 2 yrs.	11 - 14	(including naps)
3 - 5 yrs.	10 - 13	(including naps)
6 - 12 yrs.	9 - 12	
13 - 18 yrs.	8 - 10	

* * * These are just recommendations. Every child is different, and each person's need for sleep varies.

That's a lot of sleep, and without it, a child's green zone shrinks and his windows of tolerance narrow, leaving him vulnerable to becoming more and more emotionally volatile and less able to regulate himself and even problem-solve.

This is no surprise to you—your own kids become more reactive and less balanced and resilient when they're tired and behind on sleep. That's why you may feel dread of a lurking, ominous, oncoming grumpiness when your kids ask to spend the night with a friend. Dealing with overtired, short-fused blue- or red-zone kids on a Saturday or Sunday afternoon is pretty much a universal parenting experience.

But it's not only sleepovers that cause sleep problems for kids and produce blue- and red-zone moments. Here are some other factors that get in the way of sleep:

- *A schedule that's too full.* Consider whether too many activities are backing up your family's bedtime and eating into kids' sleeping hours. (We'll discuss specific suggestions in the following Yes Brain strategy.)
- *A chaotic or noisy environment.* A home or neighborhood that stays active and raucous or siblings who have different bedtimes but share a room can create challenges for parents committed to getting their kids consistent sleep. These circumstances might not be anything you can easily change. In that case you may need to be creative by blocking out light, moving kids to their rooms once they fall asleep, or using white noise to drown out sound.
- *Parental work hours.* A child's sleep can be compromised when a parent can't get home in time to eat dinner and help with homework until later hours. Again, if these are circumstances that can't be shifted, you may need to get creative, maybe even having siblings or neighbors help with homework or having young kids eat earlier during the week and then have the parent just arriving from work go in for story time and eat dinner after that. Every family will have to see what works best for them.
- *Bedtime power struggles.* When the context around hitting the sack becomes contentious, stressful, angry, or fearful, the brain wires a negative association with sleep and the

whole bedtime routine, so kids will often resist it even more. Instead, we want to create positive associations with sleep, so that children view it as safe, relaxing, and even connecting, as opposed to stressful and combative. You might need to redesign your bedtime routine with more time allowed for reading, snuggling, and staying present. *Emphasizing connection almost always ends up leading to children falling asleep more quickly and peacefully, so parents get more time to themselves and spend less time battling with their kids.*

- *Not enough time to "ramp down."* The more we learn about kids, the more we understand how important it is to address the needs of an individual's nervous system. Especially when it comes to sleep, parents need to allow for the body and nervous system to settle. We don't just go from awake to asleep—there is a process of "downregulating" in which our nervous system starts to slow down to allow us to move into sleep. We need to prime the brain and give it time to shift to lower and slower states of bodily arousal so children can fall asleep.

This relationship between sleep and balance applies not only to kids, of course. Think about your own experiences. When you get less sleep, don't you have a less-balanced brain? Aren't you less patient, less able to regulate your own emotions? The difference is that adults have had years to practice maintaining control even when we're tired. We're not always good at it, but we've got fully developed brains and have had more opportunities to try to improve in this area. We're typically more aware of our shortcomings when we're sleep-deprived and can monitor ourselves better. Kids, though, can move quickly toward the red or blue zone, and they haven't fully developed the skills to move back into the green zone as easily on their own. So think about ways you can maximize the ZZZ's for your kids during the nighttime, so they can enjoy more emotional balance and behavioral regulation during the day.

Yes Brain Strategy #2 for Promoting a Balanced Brain: Serve a Healthy Mind Platter

As you probably know, the U.S. Department of Agriculture has replaced its food pyramid with a needed revision, a "choose my plate" pictorial example of a dish that includes all the food groups (fruits, vegetables, protein, grains, and dairy) to remind us of what a daily diet should consist of to optimize physical health.

When it comes to creating healthy mental and emotional balance within your kids, what would be the equivalent of recommended daily servings for a strong and balanced mind? What experiences promote integration and help kids (and adults) connect parts of the brain and join members of a family and community, honoring differences and promoting compassionate linkages with one another?

To address these questions, Dan and David Rock, a leader in the organizational consulting world, created what they've called the Healthy Mind Platter, consisting of seven daily essential mental activities (including play and sleep, which we've highlighted earlier) to optimize brain matter and create balance and well-being:

Focus time: When we closely focus on tasks in a goal-oriented way, we take on challenges that make deep connections in the brain.

Play time: When we allow ourselves to be spontaneous or creative, playfully enjoying novel experiences, we help make new connections in the brain.

Connecting time: When we connect with other people, ideally in person, and when we take time to appreciate our connection to the natural world around us, we activate and reinforce the brain's relational circuitry.

Physical time: When we move our bodies, aerobically if medically possible, we strengthen the brain in many ways.

Time-in: When we quietly reflect internally, focusing on sensations, images, feelings, and thoughts, we help to better integrate the brain.

Down time: When we are non-focused, without any specific goal, and let our mind wander or simply relax, we help the brain recharge.

Sleep time: When we give the brain the rest it needs, we consolidate learning and recover from the experiences of the day.

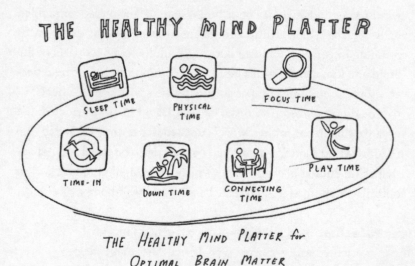

THE HEALTHY MIND PLATTER for OPTIMAL BRAIN MATTER

Based on the Healthy Mind Platter, copyright © 2011 David Rock and Daniel J. Siegel

These seven daily activities make up the full set of "mental nutrients" that your brain and relationships need to function at their best. By giving a child opportunities every day in each of these servings, you promote integration in her life and enable her brain to coordinate and balance its activities. These essential mental activities strengthen her brain's internal connections and her networks with other people and the world around her. Too much or too little of any of these endeavors over time can be problematic.

So our second Yes Brain strategy for promoting a balanced brain is to make sure that your child's experiences and schedule are delivering the various needs represented in the Healthy Mind Platter. For example, your kids might get plenty of focus time at school, along with lots of play time and connecting time. And maybe they enjoy physical time when they attend dance classes and play sports. But when you look at your family's typical schedule for a week, you might notice that your children aren't getting much down time or time-in, or maybe you'll notice that they're not getting enough sleep time.

Or it could be that you have a more introspective child who spends plenty of time being quiet and focused and enjoys a good amount of time-in. But maybe he needs more physical time moving his body, or more connecting time playing with friends or eating meals with the rest of the family.

Or maybe you're asking for too much focus time from your kids by emphasizing grades so much that it's hard for them to spend a healthy amount of time on the other activities on the platter. Be mindful of the fact that it's the rare child who will get all A's or execute every assignment perfectly. If you emphasize academic excellence and achievement over everything else, your child may feel that whatever she does is never quite good enough. The child psychologist and author Michael Thompson shares that he's heard from many kids and teenagers that their parents care more about their grades than they care about them. The overall focus is on a fixed destination rather than on the journey of discovery, more about the outcome than the effort. No wonder we see so many adolescents with rising levels of anxiety and depression, and fewer connected relationships to help moderate these feelings.

Except for loose guidelines on sleep above, we're not recommending specific amounts of time for each activity on the Healthy Mind Platter. There's not an exact recipe for a healthy mind, since each individual is different and our needs change over time. The point is to become aware of the full spectrum of mental activities and, as with essential nutrients, do your best to bring the right ingredients into your kids' mental diet, ideally for at least a bit of time each day. Just as you wouldn't want them to eat only pizza every day for days on end, we wouldn't provide them with only focus time, with little time for sleep. The key, once again, is *balancing* the day with these essential mental activities. Balance and mental wellness are all about reinforcing our connections with others and the world around us, and strengthening the connections within the brain itself.

We realize, by the way, that a real commitment to balance in your child's life can feel a bit scary. It's tough sometimes to choose *not* to follow along in the direction the others in your community are going. It can feel threatening to cut back on extra tutoring or enrichment classes and simply trust the process, allowing your child to develop in his own direction. But do try to give yourself permission to go beyond a narrow definition of success for your kids. Permission to talk to your child's school about homework load. Permission to step off the treadmill of "success" and do what's best for your child and for your family.

Thus the Healthy Mind Platter. When we vary the focus of attention with this spectrum of mental activities, we give the brain lots of opportunities to develop in different ways. Time spent playing or working or reflecting or connecting fills the day, yes, but it also teaches and builds skills. When we set the stage for time for each of these, not only are we giving the brain opportunities to fire and wire for a wider range of mental activities that our kids are capable of, but we're wiring the rhythm and feel of a balanced life for them as well. Simply by remaining aware of the Healthy Mind Platter and teaching your kids about it, you can create an appetite for balance and mental well-being each day.

Yes Brain Kids: Teach Your Kids About Balance

The idea of a balanced brain is a concept we can teach our children. And the conversations you have with them about balance, and the Yes Brain state in general, will help them understand basic concepts regarding mental and emotional health. Plus, the more they understand the importance of overall balance—of the mind as well as of the family schedule—the better they will be able to articulate when they feel out of balance.

To help get you started, we've offered here a "Yes Brain Kids" section you can read with your children to help teach them about their own Yes Brain. We'll do this at the end of each of the following chapters. We've written these sections with five- to nine-year-olds in mind, but you should feel free to adapt them to fit the age and developmental stage of your own kids.

Yes Brain Kids: Teach Your Kids About Balance

You know how you feel when it just seems like everything is going right and you handle yourself well? We call this being in the green zone.

But sometimes you get upset. You might get really mad, or maybe scared or nervous. You might want to cry or yell. This is what we call being in the red zone.

Or maybe when you get upset you pull away from everyone, wanting to be quiet and by yourself. Maybe your body feels limp, like a noodle. This is called going into the blue zone.

Here's a simple strategy you can use whenever you're upset and want to move back into the green. Just put one hand on your chest and one hand on your stomach. Try that now, and just sit there breathing, with a hand on your chest, and a hand on your stomach. See how calm you feel?

Now, tonight, when you're getting sleepy and your eyelids are getting heavy and your body is starting to feel relaxed, practice this trick again. Then each night, just before bed, practice it again, and notice how calm it makes you feel.

Yes Brain Kids: Teach Your Kids About Balance

Olivia used this strategy when her friends at school didn't invite her to play with them. It hurt to be left out, and she felt herself entering the blue zone. She started to cry, and just wanted to disappear.

But she noticed the blue zone feelings and calmed herself by putting her hands over her heart and stomach. She felt better right away and moved back into the green zone. She still felt a little sad, but she knew she'd be okay.

The next time something makes you feel sad, or angry, or afraid, use this tool. With practice, you'll get to where you can use it at any time to help you move back into the green zone when you need to.

My Own Yes Brain: Promoting Balance in Myself

Take a moment right now to think about how balanced you feel in your own life. Here are three questions to help you explore your own sense of balance. You might even want to journal a bit in response, or maybe talk to another parent about how these questions affected you.

1. Think about your own green zone. How easily do you leave it, and how hard is it to return once you've entered the red or the blue zone? Consider these questions generally, for sure, but focus primarily on your experiences with your children. Do you live mostly in the green or red or blue?

2. Consider how integrated you are in your relationship with your kids. Are you too *differentiated without linkage*, leaving your children to fend for themselves emotionally? Too *linked without differentiation*, leading to enmeshment? What percentage of the time do you live in the integration sweet spot, where you stay emotionally connected to and supportive of your kids while still giving them space to be individuals (as appropriate given their age and individual temperaments)?

3. How's your own Healthy Mind Platter? Look at the platter again, but this time think specifically about your own individual daily schedule, and how you spend your time and energy.

With that in mind, take a few minutes now and draw your own platter, considering how you spend the majority of your time. Just draw a circle and divide it up like a pie chart into twenty-four wedges, one for each hour of the day. How many hours each day do you spend on sleep, physical time, connecting time, and so on? It might look something like the platter on the next page.

When you think of the hours in your day, which of the Healthy Mind Platter activities is consistently getting short shrift? We don't mean to be unrealistic here. Parents, by definition, are people whose circumstances don't easily lend themselves to a healthy allocation of time. This is especially true if you have really young children. In that case, you may have trouble even finding time to eat and go to the bathroom, much less get enough sleep and time for reflection (or for drawing your own platter). We get it. We've been there ourselves.

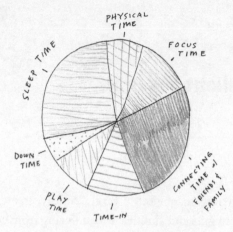

But it's still helpful to assess how well you're doing at maintaining some semblance of balance in your life, no matter how unrealistic it might feel right now. The very act of seeing what you're missing out on—whether that's sleep, exercise, time alone, down time, or any of the other necessary daily activities in the Healthy Mind Platter—can offer perspective on the personal needs that are going unmet right now, and at least give you the chance to consider how better to meet them going forward. Our own balance is essential to our own green zones being robust so that we can be who our kids need us to be.

Again, a balanced brain isn't always easy to achieve when you're responsible for the welfare and development of your children. But the more you can aim for balance and create a Yes Brain within your-self, the more you'll be able to do the same for the ones in your care.

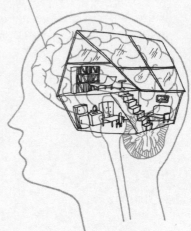

CHAPTER 3

The Resilient Yes Brain

lanah was an obviously bright nine-year-old who, despite evident gifts and abilities, was suffering from consistent anxiety. She worried about everything: tests at school, social interactions, global warming, whether her mom would die, and the health of her guinea pig. Her parents took her to see Tina when, eventually, the anxiety showed up as intense panic attacks that interfered with regular activities and caused her a lot of distress. To make things worse, she was dealing with chronic health issues that experts were telling her were "all psychological."

As Tina spent time getting to know Alanah, she discovered that her young client naturally was highly conscientious and tended toward perfectionism as part of her personality; she "ran anxious" in most areas of her life. Tina recognized this anxiety spiral, where Alanah would fixate on a possible challenge, then have trouble handling that challenge, then worry because she didn't handle it well. For example, one day she forgot her lunch at home. She worried about the embarrassment of not having food when her friends ate, then she began to worry about being so hungry that she wouldn't be able to listen well in class, which meant she wouldn't understand the homework, which would lead to a poor performance on the next test. It became so intense that she began regularly hiding out in the bathroom at school for long periods of time while she was in the middle of a panic attack. Like so many of her fears, this typical childhood experience—forgetting her lunch at home—led to a cycle that became increasingly incapacitating. This anxiety spiral was creating a No Brain, a neuronal firing state in Alanah that left her paralyzed virtually any time she faced an obstacle or experienced even a minor setback.

Later in the chapter we'll come back to Alanah's story and explain Tina's approach in this case, and how she helped her move back toward an integrated brain and a receptive state, a Yes Brain. First, though, we want to introduce you to the second of the four fundamentals of the Yes Brain—resilience.

In Chapter 2 we talked about helping kids become more balanced so they can do a better job of remaining in the green zone. Now we'll look at encouraging resilience and grit in our kids, which is about not only staying in the green zone but *expanding and strengthening* it. The wider their window of tolerance for difficult times and uncomfortable emotions, the more resilient they can be in the face of adversity, instead of falling apart when things don't go their way. Resilience is also about bouncing back, about how readily they are able to move from the red or blue zone back into the green zone—how they can return from chaos or rigidity and get back into the harmony within the window.

In a No Brain state, kids experience fear, dread, and reactivity, intimidated by unforeseen complications and unable to maintain control over their own bodies, emotions, and decisions. We want them, instead, to develop Yes Brain resilience and know that they have the skills—or can learn the necessary skills—that will help them face adversity with grit and bounce back from defeats. They can then more fully experience real and lasting success in their lives—whether they have worries and anxieties, like Alanah, or are simply kids growing up in our stressful, fast-paced, high-expectation world where life doesn't always go as planned.

The Goal: Skill-Building Instead of Extinguishing Unwanted Behavior

Let's begin by thinking about how best to respond when kids behave in unpleasant ways. Many parents assume that the goal is to extinguish unwanted behavior, to make it stop or go away. But remember, behavior is communication. And problematic behavior is actually a message, where our kids are saying, "I need help building skills in this certain area. I can't do this well yet." So the primary focus, when our kids are struggling, should be not on getting rid of bad behavior or extinguishing red-zone chaos and blue-zone rigidity, but on figuring out what we want to add—the skills to handle things better next time. *Of course* we want to minimize problematic behaviors. All parents do. (Believe us, we've both wanted to get rid of lots of our own kids' behaviors at every stage.) After all, any time our kids are out of control, it's hard on them, on us, and on the whole family. But if we want to help kids develop a Yes Brain, we need to focus less on extinguishing the problematic behavior and more on helping children *build skills* so that they can learn to move back into the green zone, preferably on their own.

> The primary focus, when our kids are struggling, should be not on getting rid of bad behavior or extinguishing red-zone chaos and blue-zone rigidity, but on figuring out what we want to add—the skills to handle things better next time.

The more we can help them develop the skills they need to avoid leaving the green zone in the first place and to move themselves back into the green zone when things don't go their way, the more they'll be able to exist in a state of equilibrium and well-being—which of course will make life more enjoyable for them, as well as for you and the whole family. That's the equanimity aspect of happiness the Greeks called *eudaimonia*. Equanimity doesn't mean someone is always calm—it means that they've learned to ride the waves of their emotions with skill and agility. If they tip over, they've learned the skill of how to get back on and surf. Resilience is a gift we can give our kids that keeps on giving. As the old saying goes, give a man a fish and he eats for a meal; teach a man to fish and he eats for a lifetime.

Instead of trying to extinguish bad behavior . . .

Build skills that lead to resilience and well-being

One mom we know used this "behavior is communication" concept to skillfully handle an issue that came up with her four-year-old son, Jake. His teacher called to say that Jake was consistently experiencing conflict with his classmates. Whenever the kids took a ball to the playground, Jake would inevitably get frustrated about having to wait his turn and would grab the ball and kick it over the fence into the street. Or when the kids played tag, Jake would often become angry and even aggressive when he was tagged.

If his mom had viewed the issue from more of an extinction lens, she might have promised rewards or threatened punishment to keep Jake from acting so impulsively and antagonistically when he didn't get his way. That's the approach parents and teachers most often take: they try to snuff out the bad behavior using purely behavioral approaches such as sticker charts or other carrots and sticks.

This mother, however, viewed her son's situation through a Yes Brain lens and recognized that Jake's actions were communicating the skills he lacked: namely, that he wasn't very good at sharing and taking turns, and that he didn't yet know how to be a good sport. That didn't mean he was bad. It didn't mean he was "a problem." It simply meant that his mom needed to find ways to give him practice waiting his turn and improving his ability to play well with others. So she and his teacher talked, and they came up with quick and easy ways to give him that practice—like involving Jake in the planning of the activity, role-playing where he took turns pretending to be his teacher, and having Jake help make up stories about sharing and taking turns using dolls and action figures ("Jake, help me teach Batman how to share with his friend").

The same approach can be effective with older kids as well. If your eleven-year-old wants to go to sleep-away camp with her friends but is terrified about being away from home overnight, then she's communicating that she needs some skill-building in the area of tolerating separation from you. A few sleepovers with friends or grandparents might be in order to help her build resilience in this area. Contrast this with a No Brain approach of telling her, "You have nothing to be worried about. You're big enough now to do this." The problem with this well-intentioned approach is that she actually *does* worry, and she *doesn't* feel big enough. So this response explicitly denies her feelings, leaving her confused and less able to trust her ability to read her own internal clues, and with nothing she can do to feel better. What's more, it misses an opportunity to build skills that can serve her for a lifetime.

Instead of merely focusing on extinguishing the problem

View behavior as communication and focus on building skills

When we see our children's behavior as communication that's letting us know which skills and strategies they still need to build and develop, then our responses can be more intentional and compassionate, not to mention more effective. That's because this perspective allows us to see our kids as *needing our help* and *having a hard time*, rather than just acting out and making things hard on us. This way of thinking stokes trust-based parenting, where we trust that as we build skills and allow development to unfold, our kids' brains will develop the kinds of connections that will produce resilience and help them grow into the kind of people who lead rich, happy, meaningful lives.

Resilience, Receptivity, and Expanding the Green Zone

Let's think about what developing resilience means, practically. One helpful view is that it's being resourceful in approaching life's challenges and moving through them with strength and clarity. It all goes back to reactivity versus receptivity. Reactivity blocks resilience; receptivity promotes it. So if you want to help your kids learn to handle adversity in a healthy, mature way, the first thing you need to do is help them build receptivity.

REACTIVITY blocks RESILIENCE

RECEPTIVITY promotes it

A child who is reactive is at the mercy of her surroundings; all she can do is react. Receptivity, though, allows her to observe and assess the input from her surroundings, then be proactive in how she responds. She can *choose* her response and act intentionally, rather than automatically reacting without a conscious decision on her part. That's what happens in the green zone.

That's why we say our short-term goal is to help kids become more balanced and remain in their green zone when they get upset. In the green zone they are receptive, so their learning circuitry is engaged, which means they can think and listen and understand, learn to make good decisions, consider consequences, and think about the feelings of others. Notice that with balance it's possible to feel big emotions but remain with clear thinking and cooperative communication. To put it differently, in the green zone kids can become emotional and still remain balanced, so they can much more easily access their upstairs brain. A well-developed upstairs brain and a big, hardy green zone are the keys to facing setbacks and adversity from a balanced perspective.

Thus our long-term goal is to *expand* the green zone over time. This is where building resilience comes in.

SHORT-TERM GOAL: BALANCE
(getting back into the green zone)

LONG-TERM GOAL: RESILIENCE
(expanding the green zone)

We want to widen a child's window of tolerance for dealing with difficulty, so that she's more and more capable of handling hardship and adversity. A narrow green zone makes a child more likely to become chaotic or rigid more easily, more frequently, and more intensely. The objective isn't to get rid of the red-zone and blue-zone moments altogether. In fact, there are times it's necessary and important to shift into the red or blue zones—in moments of danger or other situations when our adaptive survival responses to an actual threat are required. But we want children to be more and more able to determine when it's appropriate to exit the green zone, and to live the majority of their lives there in that calm and clear-minded place. That's what it means to expand the green zone.

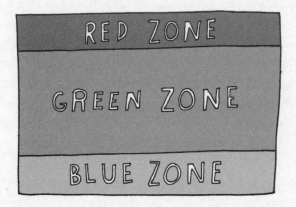

Part of widening the window of tolerance is allowing kids to face adversity, to feel disappointment and other negative emotions, and even to fail. That's how they develop grit and perseverance. If you've read any of our other books, you know that we're big believers in the importance of setting boundaries for kids, and in helping them learn how to deal with not having things go their way all the time. A huge part of developing a resilient Yes Brain involves teaching kids that difficult moments and hard times will inevitably occur. Then, instead of rescuing or protecting them from any difficult emotion or situation, we walk through those hard times *with them* and help them develop the resilience to learn and grow from setbacks and still make good decisions in the midst of an emotional tempest. We want them to internalize our message: "I'm right here with you. You've

> Part of widening the window of tolerance is allowing kids to face adversity, to feel disappointment and other negative emotions, and even to fail. That's how we expand their green zone: by lovingly teaching them that they can live with and then move through frustration and failure, coming out stronger and wiser on the other side.

got this. I know it's hard, but you can do it. I'm here." That's how we expand their green zone: by lovingly teaching them that they can live with and then move through frustration and failure, coming out stronger and wiser on the other side.

Expanding the green zone might involve simple actions on your part:

Expand the Green Zone

Or it might involve more complex or painful issues. After inform-
ing your seven-year-old that a beloved pet has died, your next move
might be sitting with him and holding him while he cries and talks
about all the things he loved about the pet. Or when your twelve-
year-old's best friends inform her that she is no longer popular
enough to sit with them at lunch, you'll have to resist the urge to call
the other parents or someone at school and demand she be included.
Instead, you'll just be present with your daughter and let her feel your
love and support while she aches in a new way she hasn't experienced
before, then help her do some problem-solving.

There are times, in other words, that we have to allow our kids to
hurt, and even fail, without rescuing them and depriving them of
those valuable, resilience-building lessons. And when we're emotionally present and offer our comfort in these moments, we do even
more to expand their green zone. Within their memory systems,
such experiences teach kids that things can be tough but that they
can handle it and bounce back. The next time a difficult situation
arises, part of the memory that will be activated will be these experiences of facing challenges and moving effectively through them.

Pushin' and Cushion: When to Let a Child Struggle

When we speak to parents about expanding the green zone, the same
question invariably comes up: *Yeah, but how do I know when to let my
child struggle and when to step in and help?*

For us, it comes down to a great phrase Tina heard from one of
her students: pushin' and cushion. At times our kids need us to challenge them to go beyond themselves. To remove their self-imposed
bubble wrap and ask them to risk facing circumstances and challenges they're not used to. That's the *pushin'* part: challenging them
and allowing them to develop resilience and strength and toughness
and grit. The point, obviously, is really all about "pushing the enve-
lope" of their abilities, not literally pushing their bodies to do something. It's a way to expand their green zone, to practice moving

beyond what's comfortable. When we step in and rescue a child from a problem she can handle on her own, we short-circuit her opportunity to learn how to address a difficult issue or understand her capacity to handle hard stuff. Having to visit with a teacher or address a problem with a friend can be a powerful learning opportunity. Give your child the benefit of gaining practice using her voice and her logic. Pushin' means you teach her to assert herself and to understand that she can be both respectful *and* strong, even when it makes her nervous to take a stand or face a new challenge. They learn they can do something when they do it!

> When we step in and rescue a child from a problem she can handle on her own, we short-circuit her opportunity to learn how to address a difficult issue or understand her capacity to handle hard stuff.

But only if it doesn't cause so much distress that it floods their nervous systems, sending them into the red or blue zones. If we push them too much before they're ready, when their nervous systems experience distress that is *too* uncomfortable, it can backfire, making them more fearful and more dependent, and even less willing to expand, in fact shrinking their green zone. So there are other times when our children genuinely need us to provide a *cushion*. They're facing an obstacle too big or a challenge they simply can't address by themselves. They truly can't handle the issue alone. Maybe your three-year-old isn't ready yet to sit with the other kids for lunch at the group playdate at the park and needs you to sit with him off to the side until he's ready to join the others. Or maybe your third-grader feels terrified to go to sleep by herself because of the scary image she saw on the Halloween billboard that afternoon, so she needs you to stay with her until she drifts off. Or maybe your middle-schooler's history teacher is giving so much homework that he's missing activities and losing sleep, so you feel it's necessary to step in and get more details. We shouldn't ask children to go through something alone if it's beyond their capacity to do so. So when they face a challenge that's too big to handle alone, we fiercely support them. Whereas at times we push, asking them to do more than they're comfortable with, at times like these we provide the cushion, letting them know that we're on their side, that we've got their back.

Keep in mind that the brain is an association machine, so we can try to anticipate whether pushin' would lead to their brain associating taking the uncomfortable leap with good feelings ("I did it!" or "That wasn't so bad, and I kinda had fun") or if pushin' would lead to a negative association that will make it even less likely they will want to try something next time. If you think it is likely to be a negative experience that will be too much for your child, try a little cushion, with some smaller baby steps toward the goal.

Sometimes parents need to provide the pushin' . . .

And sometimes kids need more cushion

So how do we strike the Goldilocks balance and find the porridge that's neither too hot nor too cold? How do we find what is "just right"? In other words, how do we help our kids face just enough adversity, without expecting more than they can handle? When are we supposed to provide the pushin' and when the cushion?

Well, it's not easy. Here's the way we explain it to the parents we see in our offices. We encourage them to ask themselves five questions.

Questions to help determine whether your child needs pushin' or cushion

1. *What is your child's temperament and developmental stage, and what does he or she need right now?*

    Keep in mind that your child might feel emotionally and even physically distressed when facing difficult situations. What might seem like a baby step to you can feel to your child like a dive from a towering cliff. Sometimes a child needs more baby steps, or more practice, or more time, or more cushion from you. At other times, the very same child can handle the discomfort and might need more pushin'. Stay focused on how your child responds and what that exposes about her needs in this moment. Attune to your child's actual internal experience, revealed by her signals and communication, not what you *think* she should be feeling.

2. *Are you clear on what the real issue is?*

    What elements are causing your child to resist facing this obstacle or dealing with this particular challenge? You might assume that a sleepover is scary because she will have to be away from you, but it might have more to do with embarrassment related to her fear that she might wet the bed. Or maybe you think a reticence about joining the swim team has to do with an unwillingness to exercise and work hard, but it might have more to do with a fear of wearing a Speedo in public. So talk to your child and get clear on what the real issue is. Then you can help problem-solve.

3. *What messages do you send about risk-taking and failure?*

As an adult, you already understand the importance of facing fears and of being willing to try and fail. You know how much we learn when we take a leap and when we mess up, and you realize that every mistake is an opportunity for growth and self-understanding. But are you passing along to your kids this important life lesson? What explicit and implicit messages do you send about taking risks? About "being careful"? About divergent thinking? About whether "failure" is ever acceptable? Do you send messages about doing everything just right or perfectly, where your kids might not feel freedom to color outside the lines? Is an "oops" ever embraced as a learning opportunity in your family? We know one dad who, when he drops off his somewhat cautious nine-year-old at school each day, tells him, "Take a chance today!" And while this message wouldn't be appropriate for every child, for this guarded and thoughtful boy it's just the kind of message that can lead to a Yes Brain mentality. We learn from taking chances and making mistakes, so we can take another chance and try again. A Yes Brain fosters courage, empowering us to realize that, whether with another's help or on our own, we can always be open to more learning.

4. *Does your child need skills to handle potential (and inevitable) failure?*

Again, the goal isn't to protect your children from failure but to help build skills that lead to overcoming adversity. One such skill is the ability to recognize that surmounting obstacles is often part of a long process. In other words, something being difficult doesn't mean there is something wrong with you. So one of the best lessons to teach our kids is psychologist Carol Dweck's concept of "yet." When kids say "I can't do it" or "I'm not ready," just have them add the word "yet." This promotes an attitude of possibility that offers tremendous power because it works from a Yes Brain state and the idea that they *will* be able to succeed and achieve, as long as they're willing to prepare themselves, to persist, and to work toward that success.

5. *Are you giving your child tools to help return to and expand the green zone?*

One of the most important skills to build within your kids is the ability to calm themselves down and regain control once they've moved into the red or blue zone. One quick and powerful tool we discussed earlier is to have them place a hand on their chest over their heart and a hand on their belly and take some slow, deep breaths. Just this can be a great tool for calming distress. Then they can make wiser—and braver—decisions about which challenges to take on. (We'll discuss more such skills below, and later in the book.)

Reflecting on these questions can help you be more mindful about where your child is—and where you are—as you decide whether to offer pushin' or cushion in response to a difficult moment. Being mindful includes being aware of what's happening inside you, as well as being open and receptive to what's going on inside your child. It begins with an intentional state of mind, one that purposefully focuses on your child's particular needs for encouragement or guidance. We want to be as intentional and thoughtful as possible in responding to our kids when they're upset. Children vary in their tolerance of fear, challenge, and risk. Some kids happily jump into new and difficult situations headfirst, and even delight in solving problems and overcoming obstacles. Other kids feel really uncomfortable taking chances and trying something unknown or challenging. And often the very same child will respond one way at one time and differently at another. They're predictably unpredictable at times. So remember that every child is different and complex. In each situation, make decisions about what's best for this unique child in this particular moment, and what will lead to growth and an expansion of what they believe they can do. That's resilience.

What You Can Do: Yes Brain Strategies That Promote Resilience

Yes Brain Strategy #1 for Promoting a Resilient Brain: Shower Your Kids with the Four S's

As with just about anything else when it comes to parenting, relationship is the key to building resilience. A powerful predictor for resilience and how well a child turns out, in terms of optimizing social, academic, and emotional functioning, is whether that child experienced secure attachment with at least one person—a parent, grandparent, or other caregiver. That's right: by giving your kids predictable (not perfect), sensitive care, where they feel connected and protected, you'll give them the chance to be not only happier and more fulfilled, but more successful emotionally, relationally, and even academically.

This kind of connected care offers kids what's called secure attachment, where they experience the four S's.

Shower Your Kids
with the Four S's

$\underline{S}$afe

$\underline{S}$een

$\underline{S}$oothed

$\underline{S}$ecure

The four S's are about helping kids feel safe and protected, especially when they are in distress. It's about letting them know that you will keep them safe, and that you see them and love them at a deep level—even when you don't like the way they've acted. It's about soothing them and helping calm them when they're upset. And it's about creating a feeling of deep security about their lives—because they feel safe, seen, and soothed. Neurologically, these repeated secure attachment experiences allow the brain to connect up in optimal ways and lead to a well-developed upstairs brain, allowing kids to feel more secure in every aspect of their lives. When we consistently (but not perfectly) provide the four S's, we expand kids' green zones, meaning they're more and more capable of handling problems on their own.

One reason is fairly obvious: when your kids know that you've got their back—that you're behind them and will support and love them always—that creates the safety they need and rely on. That strong attachment relationship creates a safe base from which they can venture into the unknown, knowing that if things get too hard, they can always return and you will be there for them. That's how they develop the confidence and grit to step out of their comfort zone and try something new, uncomfortable, and even scary.

Another reason a strong parent-child relationship leads to resilience is that when you spend consistent time with your kids, you get to know them at a deep level. As a result, you become attuned to recognizing signs—both emotional and physical—that your child is moving toward the outer limits of her green zone and needs help returning to the center. It might be that your child is an *internalizer*. Maybe you see her withdrawing or avoiding social contact, which you recognize as an indication that she's perhaps feeling uneasy and the "withdraw" circuits are being activated. Or perhaps she's being hard on herself. Whatever the reasons, she may be shutting down, becoming rigid, and heading into the blue zone. Or your child may be more of an *externalizer*, who, as opposed to the more passive, inner-directed experience of the internalizer, acts out instead of collapsing inward. Maybe he throws a tantrum, yells, shows disrespect, or acts aggressively. These are obvious signs that he's moving into chaos, transitioning into the red zone.

Because of your close relationship with your kids, in other words, you have the ability to observe what they need in a given moment.

You can be mindfully present to the shifts taking place, and decide how to respond. You can determine how much pushin' or cushion is necessary in a given situation, and whether to step in right away or hold back and allow your child to remain in the frustration and adversity a bit more, so the green zone can continue to expand.

Making a good call regarding when to push and when to provide cushion may at first feel a bit overwhelming. But with a little practice, and some trial and inevitable error, we think you'll find that this way of approaching Yes Brain parenting works really well. It's like the old science saying, "Chance favors the prepared mind." Learning these fundamentals prepares your mind for the chance conditions that arise for your child—and for you—so that you are ready to tune in to their experience and provide pushin' or cushion in a natural, supportive, skill-building, and resource-developing way!

The great news about the four S's is that you're likely already making them a daily part of your interactions with your kids. All the time you're eating meals with your kids, driving them to the park, laughing together about a funny online video, and even arguing with each other and then comforting and repairing after conflict—all of these experiences deepen the bond you share with them, and all of them promote resilience and an integrated brain. In fact, if you do nothing else but provide your child the experience of feeling safe, soothed, seen, and secure most of the time, you're doing the most powerful thing you can do to build an integrated, resilient brain.

Yes Brain Strategy #2 for Promoting a Resilient Brain: Teach Mindsight Skills

One of the best ways to promote resilience—as well as virtually any other important psychological or relational quality—is to teach kids mindsight skills. "Mindsight" is a term Dan coined that means, in its simplest form, the ability to perceive and understand your own mind and the mind of others. It's a way of sensing and making sense of the inner mental life we all have. Mindsight includes three facets: insight, empathy, and integration. As we'll explain in subsequent chapters, insight focuses on understanding your own mind; it's the capacity for self-awareness and self-regulation. Empathy is about understanding the mind of another, and it allows us to see through someone else's eyes, to sense their emotion and resonate with them. And integration, as we've said, is linking differentiated parts so they can work together, whether that means in the individual brain or in relationship with others. Integration in a relationship, for example, honors differences and cultivates compassionate communication that links two or more people to each other. To have mindsight is to practice insight, empathy, and integration.

Mindsight skills, then, are tools we can use to alter our perspective on a situation and gain more control over our emotions and impulses, so we can make good moment-by-moment decisions that improve our relationships with others. By helping kids develop mindsight skills, we give them the capacity to avoid being victims of their emotions and circumstances, simply because they have some strategies to help them deal with what comes up. As a result, they can learn to use their minds and bodies to change their brains and emotions.

This is what Tina did with Alanah, the girl we told you about at the beginning of the chapter: she taught Alanah strategies to improve her personal insight and help her understand, then deal with, her fear and anxiety. Tina knew she needed to peel back the layers to figure out where Alanah's anxiety was coming from and curiously examine what was contributing to the heightened nervous system arousal that caused her frequent panic attacks. In other words, she needed to help figure out why her young client had such a narrow green zone, why she lacked balance and resilience to such an extent. But first Alanah needed some relief. She needed tools she could use to soothe herself when she felt those states of alarm taking over.

So first Tina taught her about the green zone and gave her a goal: to find ways to spend more time in her green zone, where things felt calm and safe. Then Tina began to introduce some basic mindsight tools. Every kid is different, of course, and some strategies work better than others. For Alanah, two particular tools were especially effective.

The first was the mindfulness exercise we detailed in the "Yes Brain Kids" section of Chapter 2. Tina began by asking Alanah to do something each night just before she fell asleep. Tina told her, "When you are getting sleepy and your eyelids are getting heavy and your body is starting to feel relaxed, I want you to put one hand on your chest and one hand on your stomach. Try it right now and notice how calming and soothing it feels. Just sitting here breathing, with a hand on your chest and a hand on your stomach. That's what I want you to do each night right before going to sleep." Tina then explained the technique to Alanah's mom and gave them the "assignment" to try it each night.

Every week when Alanah visited Tina's office they'd discuss the nighttime calming routine and practice it together there in the office. Within weeks, Tina began to observe that when Alanah would put her hands on her chest and her stomach, she immediately and automatically took a long deep breath. Then her muscle tone would soften, and her body would noticeably move into a relaxed state.

The first time it happened, Tina brought her attention to it: "Did you notice that? What just happened with your body?" What Tina was doing at that moment was teaching Alanah about *monitoring* what was going on inside her body. Alanah hadn't even been consciously aware of the relaxed state of calm she was moving into, but when Tina drew her attention to it, she recognized it at once. The two of them, along with Alanah's mother, talked about what was going on—about the concepts of balance and resilience. Tina explained that neurons that fire together wire together, and that this exercise had made connections in her brain to associate the sensation of her hands on her heart and stomach with calm relaxation. Those neurons were firing together, so they were then becoming wired together for memory as well as skills. Alanah immediately understood these concepts and saw how the experience of being calm before sleep would become related, in her brain, with the experience of putting her hands on her body in the same pattern.

The next step, then, was to use it when she felt anxious. Tina explained that everywhere Alanah went, she carried these amazing tools with her—her hands. And she could use them whenever she began to feel fear, anxiety, and panic. At school, at home, at a friend's house, or wherever, she could just subtly move her hands to her chest and belly and create that state of balance and relaxation anytime she needed it. Tina also taught her a basic cognitive strategy, from Dawn Huebner's *What to Do When Your Brain Worries Too Much*, in which the child imagines that there's a "worry bully" sitting on her shoulder and that she can engage in a dialogue with him. She can thank that aspect of her mind for trying to protect her from an imagined threat and for being a "checker" that's watching for danger. But she can also ask the worry bully to relax at times and be less vocal about this particular fear. Alanah liked this idea a great deal, and she and Tina had fun practicing what she might say to the worry bully.

The very next week she burst into Tina's office and, with eyes lit up and a huge smile, called out, "I did it! I stopped myself right in the beginning of a panic attack!" She told Tina the story, which was again about forgetting her lunch. She said that once she felt herself moving toward the red zone and going into an intense state of stress because of her fear, she went back to what she'd been learning: "First I did my hands and took deep breaths, and then I argued with the worry bully. I told him, 'It's no big deal! I can just borrow lunch money from Carissa. She always has extra money.'" And then she said, with a fair amount of fierceness that was all her own, "Then I told the worry bully that I just didn't need him to help me worry about my lunch money anymore!"

Obviously, the mindsight tools had proven to be particularly effective for Alanah, so the two of them celebrated this significant triumph in resilience. Then Tina offered her one additional mindsight tool that helped cement the lesson about Alanah's power to use her body and her mind to influence how her brain functions. Without ever using the term, Tina taught her the basics of neuroplasticity.

Alanah loved the snow, so on a whiteboard in her office, Tina drew a simple snowy mountain. She said to Alanah, "As your worries get bigger and bigger, you go higher and higher up this big snowy mountain. And you're at the top of this worry mountain, and you feel overwhelmed. In the past in order to come down, you've gotten into a sled at the top and you've gone down the mountain and landed in Panic Attack Land." She drew the path on the mountain and showed where it led, to Panic Attack Land at the bottom of the hill. She continued, "The next time your worries got big enough, you climbed back up to the top of the mountain, and you got in your sled and went down that same path, over and over again, landing in Panic Attack Land.

"But do you know what you did today? You were at the top of the mountain, but instead of going down that same path that leads to Panic Attack Land, you used your tools, and you picked up your sled and went down a *different* path. You found a brand-new place on the mountain! You went down a path that you had never been down before, and where you landed was I Relaxed and Had a Good Day Land."

Tina drew the new path on the hill, then went on. "And what's so cool about that is that the next time your worries get so big that you're at the top of the mountain, you're going to know that you don't have to go down the path that leads to Panic Attack Land. You might still take that path from time to time; after all, it's the path you're used to, and the rut is pretty deep. But snow is always falling, and the less you use the path to Panic Attack Land, the more it will get covered up by new snow. And the more you go down the other path, the more traveled it is and easy to follow in the future. This new path will become the one you'll be used to, and where your sled will be waiting, and you'll end up having a great day like today."

Tina brought the hopeful neuroplasticity message home by reminding Alanah about the power of her mind and body to change her actual brain. She explained that the paths on the snowy hill are like connections in our brain. They can become smaller and weaker, or bigger and stronger, depending on how much attention we give them and how much we use them. And this is just one more way we can take control of how we feel and how we respond to what happens to us.

That's the power of mindsight tools. We learn to monitor and then modify our inner experience. The reason we're such believers in mindsight tools is that they allow kids to understand and harness the power of their minds to change the way they view and respond to their circumstances. They allow them to expand their green zones. Mindsight tools allow kids like Alanah to feel anxiety and worry and still stay in the green zone instead of going to, for instance, a red panic attack. Just as Alanah began to comprehend that she didn't have to remain helpless in the face of her circumstances and fears, we want to help all kids develop a mindset that begins with the assumption that they are masters of their fate, and that even though life is hard sometimes and they don't always get what they want, they can take charge and make decisions about how they respond and who they want to be. That's resilience.

Yes Brain Kids: Teach Your Kids About Resilience

In Chapter 2's "Yes Brain Kids" section, we introduced children to the concept of the green zone and discussed what it looks like when we leave the green zone and move into the red or blue zone. In this chapter's "Yes Brain Kids," we help you promote resilience in your kids by explicitly talking with them about dealing with challenges.

The central lesson focuses on helping kids face tough situations and calm themselves down, so they don't become helpless in the face of their circumstances or emotions. You can let them know, in other words, that lots of life situations can be difficult, and that it's okay to feel challenged by what comes up, but that those difficulties can make us stronger. Here's a way to start the conversation:

Yes Brain Kids: Teach Your Kids About Resilience

Derek wanted to play Little League, but he was afraid.

His parents encouraged him, though. They even went with him to the first practice, and his mom volunteered to help coach the team.

The first practice he didn't love it, but the second practice was pretty fun. Then, in his first game he got a hit, and it turned out he had a blast. Now he loves baseball. And he wouldn't have known that if he hadn't been willing to confront his fear and try something new.

Yes Brain Kids: Teach Your Kids About Resilience

Do you ever feel nervous like Derek did about playing baseball? Do you ever feel pulled a little bit into the red zone, or maybe into the blue?

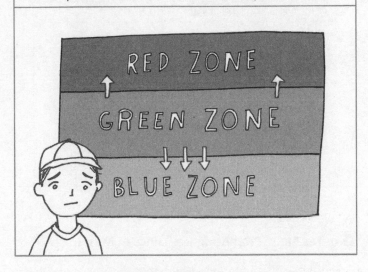

It's not easy to be brave, especially when you feel yourself outside the green zone. But sometimes, when you try something new, you find out you can do more than you realize.

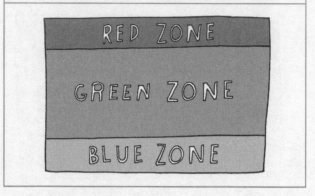

It feels really great to be brave when something is hard. Plus, it will make your green zone even bigger, and you won't miss out on new experiences you might really enjoy! You learn that you can do hard things, and that feeling uncomfortable or afraid is okay and that you can do it anyway!

RED ZONE

GREEN ZONE

BLUE ZONE

My Own Yes Brain: Promoting Resilience in Myself

Now that you've thought a good bit about developing resilience in your kids, take a moment and apply the ideas to your own life. The more we build our own Yes Brain, the more our children will be able to expand theirs.

Here are some questions to consider in reflecting on your own history of resilience and where you are at now in having a Yes Brain:

1. Have you ever noticed a pattern in terms of where you tend to go when you leave the green zone? What are the typical triggers that reveal a narrow green zone? Is the chaos of the red zone somewhere you tend to go when you feel overwhelmed, so anger or getting upset is a tendency you've experienced? Or do you move toward the rigidity of the blue zone, when you shut down either in an activated halt or in a collapsing "faint" response of falling apart? For some, the blue and red zones may be equally their go-to position when the green zone is no longer available.

2. What is the experience like for you to actually be in the red or blue zone? How long do you tend to stay there? For some, it takes

time away from an interaction to "come back online." These zones are like flipping your lid, when you've lost the integrative functioning of your prefrontal cortex we discussed in Chapter 1. In that low-road state, it may be hard for any of us to come back into the integrated, flexible Yes Brain state.

3. In the No Brain blue or red zone, what have you found is most effective to get back to the Yes Brain green zone? These are repair processes that differ for each of us, and knowing your particular strategy is a source of resilience. Some like to take a break, getting away from a situation. Others like to take a drink of water, listen to music, stretch, and reflect on what is going on. Journaling can be a helpful practice to strengthen your strategies for returning to the green zone.

4. What are your "growth edges," or the particular areas that need strengthening in your resilience resources? Are there particular themes that have restricted green zones? Are there specific situations that are especially challenging? Is monitoring your internal world to reveal signs of leaving the green zone for the rigid blue zone or the chaotic red zone something that is challenging at this point in your life? Is modulating back from blue or red toward green difficult to achieve?

5. Can you support your own growth well? This would involve seeking some help from friends, relatives, or others when needed, and building your own skills of self-regulation for different situations.

In many ways, building your own resilience is building your Yes Brain. As you do this important work, not only will you be developing the presence of mind that will serve you well, but as you model living life from a Yes Brain and approaching challenges with resilience, you will be helping your child! We all grow throughout the life span, so enjoy the journey of building these circuits of strength and well-being.

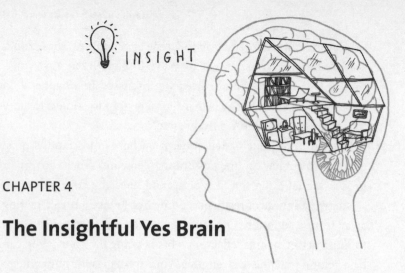

INSIGHT

CHAPTER 4

The Insightful Yes Brain

Tina was getting ready one morning when Luke, her eight-year-old, burst into the bathroom sobbing. Here's how she tells the story:

Once I helped Luke calm down enough to talk, he explained that his five-year-old brother, JP, had "five-starred" him. I didn't know this phrase, so he explained that it meant that you slap someone with an open palm so hard that it leaves a hand-print-shaped mark on the other person's skin, where the finger imprints look like the points of a star. He lifted his shirt, and sure enough, I saw the five red points of the star, shaped like a five-year-old's hand, on the skin of Luke's back.

I comforted him, then went and found his younger brother, the perpetrator, who was still obviously in the red zone. If you've heard me speak, you've likely heard one of my stories where I handled myself poorly as a parent. On this particular morning, though, I was in the green zone and mindful enough to see this discipline moment as what all discipline moments should be: a teaching situation, a time to build skills. It was a perfect time to help JP develop the third fundamental of the Yes Brain: insight.

Recognizing that he was still in a reactive, non-receptive emotional place where little learning could happen, I knew it would be more effective and attuned to connect before redirecting. I knelt and let him fall into my arms, and I comforted and calmed him by saying, "Oh, buddy. You are so mad. Come here."

As the sobbing subsided and his muscles began to soften and his mood began to calm, I said with empathy, "I know you know it's not okay to hit like that. What happened?"

In asking this question, I was implementing a strategy we detail in *The Whole-Brain Child*: "Name it to tame it." I let JP tell his version of the story, which helped him further calm down as he named how he was feeling, so he could tame his big emotions. He explained that he and Luke had been on the phone with their grandmother, and he was telling a joke. Then, just as he got to the end, Luke blurted out the punch line. After they hung up, JP tried to tell Luke how mad he was, only to have Luke tease him in response.

I sympathized with JP and let him express his immense frustration over what, to him, clearly was a breach of joke-telling etiquette so significant that it warranted the new-to-me five-star technique. Then I began using this common discipline moment—and remember, discipline is always about teaching—to build insight within my five-year-old son.

JP further calmed down as I soothed him, so I began asking questions to call his attention to his own experience, to the moment when he entered the red zone and lost control: "What did you feel in your body when that happened?" and "Was there a moment you knew you were going to explode?" I wanted to lead him to think about and better understand what had happened inside him that led to this moment.

Then the conversation could naturally transition into questions like "When you feel that anger bubbling up inside you, what else can you do to express it?" and "What works for you? What calms you down when you're really upset and your downstairs brain is taking over?" Having connected with him and begun to help build insight through our reflective dialogue, I could then move into the "redirect" phase of the conversation, where I asked what he could do to make things right with his brother.

As we explain in *No-Drama Discipline*, effective discipline—which focuses not on punishment but on teaching—aims at two primary goals: (1) getting short-term cooperation by stopping a bad behavior or promoting a good one, and (2) building skills and nurturing connections in our children's brains that will help them make better decisions and handle themselves well in the future. These were Tina's goals as she talked with JP. She achieved her first goal by connecting emotionally with her son so he could calm down and be receptive to learning. He wasn't going to learn much until she got him into the receptive green zone, where he could engage his learning circuitry. The second goal centered on helping him become more aware of his own feelings and reactions, so he could make better (and less reactive) decisions when he was upset in the future, as his development unfolded. She wanted him to become more insightful.

Building an Insightful Brain

Of all the Yes Brain fundamentals we'll discuss in this book, insight may be the one you've thought the least about. Simply put, it's the ability to look within and understand ourselves, then use what we learn to be more in control of our emotions and circumstances. And that's not easy—for kids *or* adults. But it's worth the effort required to acquire and develop it. Insight is a key element of social and emotional intelligence as well as mental health. Without it, it's practically impossible to understand ourselves and engage in and enjoy relationships with others. In other words, it's an essential requirement for living a life full of creativity, happiness, significance, and meaning. If that's the kind of life you want for your kids, teach them to be insightful.

One key aspect of insight is simple observation. Insight allows us to notice, and pay close attention to, our inner world. It's common for all of us—kids and adults—to remain unaware of what we're actually feeling and experiencing. Sometimes we become upset and immediately react, as JP did above. But other times we can become angry and don't even realize that we're mad—or we even deny it. Or we feel hurt or disappointed or resentful or insulted or jealous, and we act out of those feelings, even though we actually have no idea that we're feeling that way.

These emotions themselves aren't the problem. Don't misunderstand that. Feelings are important, even when they feel uncomfortable, or what we often name as "bad." The problem comes when we experience these various emotions but don't realize that we're doing so. When that's the case, those unacknowledged feelings can lead to all kinds of harmful and unwanted or unintended actions and decisions that we probably wouldn't make if we were simply aware of how we felt. So that's a key reason we want to develop insight. It shines the light of awareness on the emotions that are affecting us so we can *choose* how to act.

Unacknowledged feelings can lead to all kinds of harmful and unwanted or unintended actions and decisions that we probably wouldn't make if we were simply aware of how we felt.

And it's not just *feelings* that we want to remain aware of. In *The Whole-Brain Child* we gave you the acronym SIFT, which stands for sensations, images, feelings, and thoughts—the various impulses and influences you experience within yourself. We could add to that list, mentioning memories, dreams, desires, hopes, longings, and other forces at work in your mind. Insight comes from SIFT-ing through these assorted forces and paying attention to them. When we do that, we gain power over them, so that even though they may still affect us, they won't do so without our awareness, and we can work hard to guide those impulses, rather than letting them run roughshod over our lives and lead to decisions and actions that are reactive and harmful to us and to the people around us. That's why we say insight gives us power. Superpower! With insight we don't have to remain helpless in the face of our feelings and circumstances. We can look at what's going on within our internal landscape and then make conscious, intentional decisions, rather than blindly following destructive, unconscious impulses.

Insight gives us power. Superpower! With insight we don't have to remain helpless in the face of our feelings and circumstances. We can look at what's going on within our internal landscape and then make conscious, intentional decisions, rather than blindly following destructive, unconscious impulses.

The Player and the Spectator

When we talk about looking at what's going on within our internal landscape, we mean that we acknowledge and even embrace the emotions we're experiencing in the moment, while simultaneously observing our own reactions to those emotions. Scientists, philosophers, theologians, and all kinds of other thinkers have discussed this idea for centuries. Sometimes they've described it as being mindful of different planes of consciousness. Or they've talked about dual modes of processing information. Whatever the phrasing, the essential concept is that we're both feeling our feelings in the moment and watching ourselves feel those feelings. We're both observer and observed, or the experiencer and the eyewitness to the experience. To put it in terms kids can understand, we're both the player on the field and the spectator in the bleachers.

For example, imagine yourself in your car. You've just taken your kids to the movies, where you decided to splurge and actually buy the outrageously priced popcorn, rather than microwaving your own at home and smuggling in pre-packed baggies in your purse or coat pockets. (You've done that, too, right?) Now, on the way home, rather than being happy and grateful, your kids are complaining and arguing about who gets to do what first, and the noise is getting louder and louder. Maybe it's an especially hot day, and for some reason the AC in your car isn't working well. As the chaos in the backseat escalates, so do your emotions, and you begin to enter the red zone. You're flipping your lid, and you feel like you're about to really lose it. Without insight, your downstairs brain might completely take over, leading you to blow up at your kids, screaming and lecturing them about gratitude and listing the defining features of a spoiled brat.

This in-the-moment version of yourself, the one driving home from the movie, is what we'll call the "player" you—as shown in the top panel on the next page. You're in the game, on the field, right in the thick of things. And it's hard for the player to do much more than just keep playing the game and surviving whatever event pops up next.

But what if you could observe this in-the-moment, player version of yourself from a place external to the chaos? Whereas your player self is in the middle of the game and has no perspective, this observer would be the "spectator" you, simply watching the events from the stands—as shown in the bottom panel on the next page.

Can you see how a spectator in the bleachers would be able to maintain composure in a way that a player on the field couldn't? The spectator can maintain insight and perspective, even while the player is fully and frantically experiencing each present moment.

This kind of insight and perspective can come in really handy when you're in a hot car and feeling a red-zone, adult-tantrum freakout coming on as you drive your grumpy kids home from the theater. In that hot minivan you're the player in the middle of the game. But you can also imagine another, spectator version of yourself floating above the car, looking down on your player self with your kids in the backseat.

The Player and the Spectator

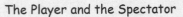

Insight lets you observe yourself so you're not a victim of your feelings and circumstances

The spectator doesn't have to be held captive by all the emotion and pandemonium in the car. Her job is simply to witness what's going on with the player. She just observes. Spectates. She doesn't judge or condemn or find fault, since she knows that feelings are important, even negative ones. She simply views the situation and notices what's going on, including how the player's anger is escalating. Whereas the in-the-moment player feels like flipping her lid and might not have any awareness of all the feelings at work within her, the spectator can mindfully SIFT through the whole situation and achieve a much fuller—and healthier—perspective on the state of affairs, sometimes even finding it amusing.

What do you think the spectator might say in this particular situation? In other words, if you could take a second as you sit there, knuckles white from gripping the steering wheel, and see yourself from a calm and peaceful position outside the current circumstances, what would you tell yourself? The spectator might say something like, "It's fine to be upset by this. Who wouldn't be? I'm only human.

But remember that the kids are tired, and so am I. They don't typically act spoiled; it just feels that way now. They're just kids. I'm going to take a deep breath and feel my body relax. Then I'm going to put on that song the kids like, and try not to say anything I'll regret, and we'll be home in a minute and can all calm down. If I need to address something about their behavior, I'll do that when we're all back in the green zone."

We're not saying this kind of insight and awareness is easy. It takes practice. But if you're willing to work at it, the simple act of observation can greatly increase the insight necessary to take control of how you behave in disturbing situations. It's so helpful!

This example is obviously about *parental* insight. But you can see how the same idea would apply to your kids as well. Understanding an idea like this requires a certain level of development and will become more achievable as children get older and more adept at sophisticated thinking. Even when your children are young, though, you can begin laying the groundwork by helping them pay attention to their feelings and the way their bodies react when they get upset. The key to insight, for adults and kids alike, is learning to pause for just a moment in the middle of a heated situation, when you take the position of the spectator. That's where the power lies: in the pause.

The Power in the Pause

Insight is all about developing and using the ability to pause in the present moment and become a spectator looking at the player, so we can gain the perspective necessary to see clearly, put things in perspective, and make sound decisions. Too often we experience a stimulus and immediately react. The noise in the hot car leads to a parental meltdown. Or an overly conscientious fourth-grader sees a difficult question on a math quiz and becomes so anxious that she has a hard time even answering the question, much less remaining calm enough to perform well on the quiz.

The Genesis of a Meltdown

When there's no pause, the reactivity takes over, and it's virtually impossible to remain in the green zone. This is how we enter a No Brain state.

If, however, we can insert one small pause, everything changes. The spectator watching you in the heated minivan steps in and reminds you to take a deep breath and get some perspective on the situation. Or when your nine-year-old feels herself freaking out about the difficult math question, a pause allows her spectator to step in and give the player version of herself the opportunity to slow her breathing and relax a bit. Again, the difference—as well as the power—rests in the pause.

Is it easy for a child to pause during a difficult moment? Of course not. Does it come naturally for most kids? No more than it does for most adults. Again, insight is a skill to be learned and practiced. For this fourth-grader to achieve this type of insight and talk herself down from her anxiety in the moment, she would need to have had adults in her life who talked to her about this skill (and modeled it), then gave her lots of opportunities to practice it. In this case, she and her father might have had various conversations about her tendency to feel nervous during tests, then worked out a "secret reminder" she could rely on when she felt the anxiety well up within her. He could teach her the importance of first noticing the fear—that's where the spectator came in—then looking to her bracelet, which would remind her of another word that begins with *br-*: breathe.

From there she could work on relaxing her shoulders and loosening her muscles, releasing the tension and anxiety that were threatening to take over. Hello, Yes Brain. And it all began with the pause, which produced the response flexibility we discussed earlier.

To put it as simply as possible, between stimulus and response we want to pause. Doing so breaks down the automaticity that comes when we immediately react to a stimulus, and allows us to make a choice about how we respond—both emotionally and behaviorally. Without the pause, and the insight that follows, there isn't a choice— it's all reaction. But when we exercise response flexibility and pause before responding, we put a temporal and mental space between stimulus and action. From a neurobiological perspective, this space of mind enables the range of possibilities to be considered. We can just "be" with an experience and reflect on it for a moment before engaging the "do" circuitry of action. Response flexibility offers us a way of choosing to be our "wisest self" possible in that moment, leading to less stress and more happiness for ourselves and the people in our lives.

Again, we realize that pausing in the middle of a heated moment is easier said than done. But you can do it. You really can. Today. And with practice, you'll get better and better at it. It may or may not ever become your default mechanism, but it will feel more and more natural as a go-to response when you face difficult situations.

Teaching Kids the Power in the Pause

What's even more exciting is that you can help your kids develop this crucial ability right now. Just as the girl taking the math quiz developed the ability to pause and calm herself down, your kids can learn to achieve insight when faced with similar obstacles. Just imagine how different their lives could be—both as children and later as teens and then adults—if they learn now to pause and make insightful choices when they face challenges! Then imagine how much more calmly and lovingly they'll be able to parent their own kids! By help-

Just imagine how different their lives can be—both as children and later as teens and then adults—if they learn now to pause and make insightful choices when they face challenges! Then imagine how much more calmly and lovingly they'll be able to parent their own kids! By helping develop insight and response flexibility in your kids when they're young, you can lay a foundation for literal generations of emotional and relational success.

ing develop insight and response flexibility in your kids when they're young, you can lay a foundation for literal generations of emotional and relational success.

We know a little girl, Alice, a first-grader, who demonstrated this Yes Brain idea beautifully. One day Alice's parents informed her that their family was going to move to a new town. Leaving her home and friends was the last thing she wanted to do, and she cried hard when her parents broke the news to her. They listened to her and let her cry. Remember, the goal of insight is *not* to short-circuit feelings. Feelings are good, and they're an important and healthy response to any stimulus. Rather than avoiding emotions, our focus is on being present to the feelings and developing insight that will produce better and healthier decisions that result from the stimulus.

Once Alice had had some time to absorb the news, she paused and decided to do what she loved to do: tell a story about the situation. She wrote the following words and made an accompanying video with the help of her dad:

Lightbulbs

Brains are important. They hold many feelings, like sad, mad, happy, playful. I think of feelings as a string of lightbulbs. When I'm happy, that string is on. When too many lightbulbs are on at once, I get confused and scared.

I feel like that now because I am moving. I feel sad and scared about moving, but I also feel a little bit excited.

If you ever feel like too many lightbulbs are on at once, sit quietly and take a deep breath. That feels good.

This is what we mean when we talk about using insight to take charge of our emotions and the way we respond to circumstances. Because she was aware of her own sadness and fear (and a little bit of excitement), Alice could pay attention to those feelings and respond in a productive and healthy manner. Notice that this story is all from the perspective of Alice as *spectator*. Alice the *player* is the one who cried, the one who felt confused and scared. That's an important aspect of herself, and she needed to remain aware of, and even embrace, that part of who she is. But because she could go to her spectator and view her situation as if from outside of herself, she could also achieve insight and perspective. This is how Alice was showing integration—she could embrace both the player and spectator part of her mind. That's the essence of integration—linking different parts of our experiences and aspects of our selves. And integration is the core of a Yes Brain. Alice could even offer advice for others who are struggling, which you see in her recommendation about sitting quietly and taking a deep breath—which of course is essentially the pause between the stimulus and the response.

Not all six-year-olds will develop this kind of Yes Brain insight, much less the ability to communicate it so clearly. Alice clearly had parents who had provided her with a strong emotional vocabulary and who had honored and given attention to her internal world. With practice, most children can improve in their understanding of themselves and their response flexibility. One boy learned from his parents the "name it to tame it" technique, and as a four-year-old he consistently used the strategy of retelling experiences to calm upsetting forces within himself.

For example, one night he spent an evening at his older cousin's house, where they watched a *Scooby-Doo* episode featuring a haunted house and frightening "ghosts" (which were, of course, tricks used by the story's villain, whose evil plan would have ultimately been successful if it hadn't been for those meddling kids—the classic *Scooby-Doo* plotline). So at bedtime the boy would tell his mother, "Mom, I need to tell the Scooby-Doo story again." He would narrate what he'd seen, and she would ask questions about details and whatever was frightening him—"And what did *that* ghost look like?"—helping him reframe his inner fears and remember that the ghosts turned out to be, as the boy put it, nothing but "this sort of shirt that was see-through and was on a zip line."

By asking to tell the story again, this young boy was demonstrating insight, recognizing from a spectator position that he needed to do something to help the player version of himself feel less scared in the moment. He was essentially demonstrating response flexibility and pausing before reacting to the stimulus of the scary images in his mind. Then the pause could lead to healthy and productive choices.

That's the kind of insight that emerges from a Yes Brain. And it's what we want to offer all of our children, so they are able to remain self-aware and monitor what's going on with their feelings and reactions. When difficult circumstances arise we want them to be able, to whatever extent their age and developmental stage will allow, to pay attention to their inner world and notice that they're becoming upset. The very act of noticing feelings of distress can then help them take charge and avoid losing control of how they feel and behave. What this means is that insight leads not only to more *understanding* of their inner world and emotions, but to more *regulation* of their feelings and behaviors as well. Regulation comes from integration. Insight creates integration by enabling us to hold in awareness the many differentiated aspects of our experience as we link them together. And this added insight-created regulation, this balance, leads to more peace and happiness for the child and the whole family.

> Insight leads not only to more *understanding* of their inner world and emotions, but to more *regulation* of their feelings and behaviors as well.

What You Can Do: Yes Brain Strategies That Promote Insight

Yes Brain Strategy #1 for Promoting an Insightful Brain: Reframe Pain

Most kids—probably most adults, too—think of struggles as inherently negative. If one choice is easier than another, then it must be better. But this is the thinking of the player, the in-the-moment part of ourselves that's just trying to survive. The spectator knows better, and that's the kind of insight we want to teach our kids. We want to reframe the pain they're experiencing so they can understand that struggles aren't always bad things to go through. Carol Dweck's notion of a growth mindset versus a fixed mindset is important here. When it comes to struggles, we can have the mindset that we can grow from effort and experience. That frame of mind gives us insight into how to approach challenges with gusto and grit—characteristics that the work of another researcher, Angela Duckworth, has shown give kids the ability to persist in the face of challenge. In contrast, a fixed mindset is where we believe that difficult situations reveal our weaknesses. We believe our innate abilities cannot be changed with effort, and so we may tend to avoid challenges in the future. We believe we should always succeed, that life should be easy.

Supporting our kids is not about giving the old "Life's not fair" lecture or preaching about the value of hard work and delaying gratification. We can teach our kids that life is about the journey of effort and discovery, not about being able to have the destination of success at our fingertips with ease. This is how we can give them the insight that supports a growth mindset. Those are all good lessons kids should learn, and there's a helpful perspective on facing difficult situations that you can encourage by asking a simple question to help develop their insight: *Which struggle do you prefer?*

Imagine, for example, that your ten-year-old loves playing goalie for her hockey team, but she hates the idea of putting in extra practice outside of her normal team activities. When you realize that this is the issue for her, you might be tempted to lecture about nothing worthwhile being easy, or about how hard work beats talent when talent doesn't work hard. But what if, instead, you simply helped her get more clear on her situation, so she could make a more informed, insightful decision? The conversation might go something like this:

DAUGHTER: Crystal always gets to play goalie, and I never do.

DAD: That's disappointing, isn't it?

DAUGHTER: Yeah. I know she's good and all, but that's just because Coach works with her after practice.

DAD: Would you like to stay after practice some and work with your coach, too? She's offered before.

DAUGHTER: But practice is already an hour and a half. That's a long time to be on skates.

DAD: I get it. So maybe think about it this way. You know how we've talked about sacrifice?

DAUGHTER: I know, Dad. I have to sacrifice if I want to be good—you've told me a thousand times.

DAD: No, that's not what I was going to say. I was just going to tell you that you're going to sacrifice either way. The good news is that you get to *choose* your sacrifice.

DAUGHTER: Huh?

DAD: Well, it'll be a sacrifice to stay and practice your backward skating and defensive skills after practice. But it's also a sacrifice if you decide *not* to put in the extra time, because then you're sacrificing the possibility that you'd improve and get to play in goal more often during the games.

DAUGHTER: I guess.

DAD: Really, think about it. I know that both options have drawbacks. But in a way, it's kind of great, because you get to *choose* what you'd rather live with. You can choose to sacrifice by putting in the extra work and maybe get to play goalie more, or you can choose to get off the ice sooner, meaning you'd rather live with less time in goal. It's totally your call.

Do you see how this father reframed the issue for his daughter? He helped her step outside of her situation and view it from the position of spectator, where she could view her options more fully. And he did so without rescuing her from making a decision or removing the discomfort involved in it. He simply helped her recognize her own agency and see that she didn't have to feel like a victim without any say in the matter. That's helping her cultivate insight.

It might take a few conversations like this before the idea really sinks in, and we're not saying that this technique will remove all frustration or self-pity in kids facing tough choices. But eventually, as she learns to go to her "spectator vision," and as she's reminded time and again that she frequently gets to choose what happens in her life, this young girl will develop more and more determination and fortitude plus a stronger and more insightful sense of self. Imagine how the ability to think in this way will serve her as she makes tough and more important decisions throughout her life!

Reframe Pain

The logic involved in preferring one sacrifice over another might be too sophisticated for very young children, but we can always be constructing the foundation for mastering the basic concept. When a three-year-old is resisting getting ready to leave, we can say, "If we're going to go see Auntie Lola, you need to get your shoes on. You were pretty excited about seeing her. Do you still want to go?" In doing so you give your toddler practice deciding between two negative alternatives (putting on shoes or missing out on time with Auntie Lola). Of course, you have to be careful with this technique, because there are plenty of times when it's not an option to, say, skip the trip to Auntie Lola's. It's not fun to have your three-year-old call your bluff and then have to come up with a way to fix the situation.

The ultimate goal, as kids move from fighting putting on their shoes to deciding about hockey practice to choosing how to approach algebra problems, is to help them become more confident in their ability to assess and understand their own feelings, to develop personal insight.

The latest research supports this reframed perspective on struggles and response flexibility. And it goes beyond just the daily struggles kids face. Even actual trauma and its effects can be mitigated by how a child views the experience. Two different people can experience the same event, and one may be traumatized and the other not. There's even a technical term—"post-traumatic growth"—to describe moments when an individual experiences profound positive transformation as a result of coping with trauma and other challenging life circumstances. Whereas some people are severely traumatized, others—some research says up to 70 percent of trauma survivors—report positive outcomes (including increased personal strength, gratitude for loved ones and life in general, greater empathy for others, and on and on) that result from the pain.

What makes the difference? Again, to a huge extent, the power's in the pause, which creates insight and allows for the *choice* of how we respond and for meaning to be created out of confusing or terrifying experiences. Insight and our perspective on a difficult event, more than the event itself, can determine how much and how positively or negatively the experience impacts our lives. Even realizing that stress in life can signify something meaningful is happening can transform how our brain interprets our body's tension, increased heart rate, and breathing. When we have the insight to reframe stress as inevitable when we care about something, it can change a negative result into a neutral or even positive one. That's why we want to reframe the pain for our kids and teach them that with practice, they can *choose* the way they look at circumstances they don't like. They can't control everything that happens to them, but with our help they can develop and practice the ability to pause before immediately reacting, become aware of what they are feeling without having to impulsively respond, and then have a choice in how they interact with their world.

Yes Brain Strategy #2 for Promoting an Insightful Brain: Avoid the Red Volcano Eruption

A practical way to teach kids about the player and the spectator is to introduce them to the Red Volcano. It's a simple concept that kids of practically any age can immediately understand, and it's based on an understanding of the way the autonomic nervous system works, which we detailed in Chapter 2. You'll remember that a hyperaroused sympathetic nervous system (which is the gas pedal that revs us up) sends us into the red zone when we become upset. It's this awareness of red-zone hyperarousal that we've found to be particularly useful when it comes to helping kids achieve insight and manage their emotions and behavior.

The idea in its simplest form is that as any of us—kids and adults alike—become upset about something, the arousal of our nervous system increases. We feel it in our bodies: our heart beats faster, our breathing increases, our muscles get tense, and our body temperature can rise. We can think of our emotional response to an upsetting stimulus as a bell curve, which with kids we call the Red Volcano.

As we become more and more upset, we move toward the top of the volcano. And that's where the danger lies, because when we reach

The Red Volcano

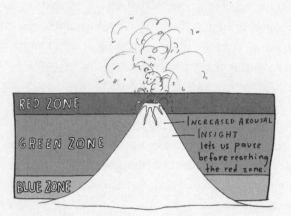

the top of the curve, we enter the red zone and erupt, losing our ability to control our emotions, decisions, and behavior. Eventually we'll "complete the curve" and come back down the other side of the mountain again, where we can reenter the green zone. But preferably, we'd never actually reach the red zone at the top of the mountain, where we lose control and erupt.

Remember, there's nothing wrong with getting upset. That's an important point we want to communicate to kids. It's good and healthy for them to feel their feelings—even and maybe especially strong ones—and to express them. This is true of uncomfortable "bad" feelings as well as for comfortable "good" feelings. And the nervous system arousal that results from these strong feelings is perfectly fine as well to be aware of and even express to others, or oneself. In fact, it's really helpful to be open and not try to stifle internal responses, because that arousal is what alerts us that we're beginning to climb the mountain and move toward eruption. The increased heart rate, shallow breathing, and tight muscles are important warning signs we need to pay attention to, and they can help us if we are in a survival situation. So we want kids to know that it's good to experience emotions, to be open to whatever their body is experiencing, but we want to help them develop the insight to recognize when their sympathetic nervous system is increasing arousal and driving them up the Red Volcano. This recognition is what will provide the powerful pause between stimulus and response. Without the pause, kids can fly straight up the mountain and into the chaotic, unmanageable red zone, where they explode.

This concept dovetails well with the player/spectator idea. Imagine, for example, you have an eight-year-old who, you've noticed, swings straight from sweet to "hangry" when he hasn't eaten in a couple of hours. Without getting into all the specifics of low blood sugar and how it affects mood, you can point out this pattern. When he's in a good frame of mind—*don't* do it when he's in the middle of a meltdown!—you can initiate the conversation by saying something like, "You know earlier, when you got so mad because you couldn't find your Dodgers hat? That's not usually the kind of thing that makes you that upset. What do you think was going on?" From there you can point out the pattern you've noticed, where he sometimes gets unusually upset when he hasn't eaten recently, and explain to him about the Red Volcano. Then teach him about the player and the spectator and how when the spectator notices the player becoming really upset, it's a good idea to grab an apple and see how it affects his mood. Again, achieving this kind of insight isn't going to be immediately easy for him, but with practice he can improve on his ability to recognize what's going on inside him, then pause and take action before he makes it to the top of the volcano. That insight will serve him well throughout his life.

And it's not only anger that we want to teach kids to recognize before it takes complete control of them. Recall the girl taking the math quiz and how she had to spot her increasing anxiety. Or imagine a child at his first sleepover who is dealing with homesickness, or one who becomes easily overwhelmed in groups and begins to shut down and refuse to interact with anyone. All of these children, with all of these emotions, need the tool of insight. They need to learn to pay attention to their own bodily and emotional sensations, then pause before reacting. They need us to teach them that in most cases they can choose to stop and change something before reaching the top of the Red Volcano.

Yes Brain Kids: Teach Your Kids About Insight

One of the best gifts we can give our kids is to help them improve their ability to *recognize* when they're moving out of the green zone and do something about it before they lose control of their upstairs brain and begin to melt down or throw a tantrum.

Yes Brain Kids

Let's talk about your feelings again, and focus on the red zone and what you can do to avoid going into the red zone in the first place. Think about your feelings as a volcano. As long as you're down low on the mountain, you're in the green zone. You feel peaceful and calm.

But when your feelings start getting really big and you get upset, you start up the mountain, toward the red zone. And guess what happens when you reach the top? You erupt!

That might mean yelling at someone, throwing an object, tearing something up, or just totally losing control.

There's nothing wrong with getting upset. But what if we could keep from reaching the top of the red volcano? What if we could catch ourselves when we began to get upset, and not ever erupt? Wouldn't it be better if we just paused and took a breath?

This is what happened with Brody. His brother, Kyle, threw a ball that hit him in the eye, and Brody was so mad! He wanted to throw something at Kyle, or say something really mean to get back at him.

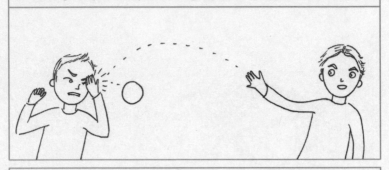

But instead he paused and took a deep breath. This is the key. He thought about the red volcano, and he made himself pause. He was still furious—just as mad as before. But he didn't act on those feelings.

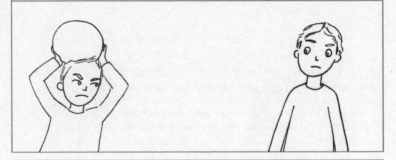

That's all you have to do when you feel yourself moving into the red zone: just pause. You don't have to stop being upset. Just pause before erupting. Then you can take a moment and think of a different response, like asking your parents for help, or telling someone how you feel.

My Own Yes Brain: Promoting Insight in Myself

You may have noticed in this chapter that, more than we usually do, we've discussed not only how to promote insight in your kids, but how important it is for a parent (or any other individual) as well. One of the most important skills you can work on—for your kids as well as yourself—is paying attention and noticing when your own frustration or fear or anger is escalating and you're beginning to move out of the green zone. Then you can pause and move to a spectator position and respond to the stimulus with insight and intentionality.

It's important to develop insight not only about what's going on in the present moment, but about what's happened in your past as well. When we work with parents, we'll often be asked some version of the question "If I had bad parents, will I be a bad parent, too?" Parents want to know whether they are doomed to repeat the same mistakes their own parents made.

Science is really clear on the answer: absolutely not. Yes, the way we were parented obviously influences the way we view the world and how we come to parent our children. But what's even more important than the specifics of what happened to us is how we've reflected on and made sense of our own childhood experiences. When we gain clear insight into our memories and how the past has influenced us in the present, we become free to construct a new future for ourselves and for how we parent our children. The research is clear: if we make sense of our lives, we free ourselves from the prison of the past and gain insight that helps us create the present and future we desire.

But what does it mean, specifically, to make sense of our lives? Dan has written about this subject throughout his career, and especially in his book *Parenting from the Inside Out*, co-authored with Mary Hartzell. If you'd like to delve deeply into this question, that's a great place to begin. But here's the basic idea. Making sense of our lives is all about developing what's called a "coherent narrative," where we reflect on and gain insight into both the positive and negative aspects of our childhood family experiences, so we can understand how these experiences led us to become who we are as adults. We're not running away from and dismissing the past, but neither are we consumed and preoccupied with it. Rather, we're free to reflect on it and choose how to respond.

For example, a section of a coherent narrative might sound something like this: "My mother was always angry. She loved us, there was never any doubt about that. But her parents had really done a number on her. Her dad worked all the time, and her mother was a closet alcoholic. Mom was the oldest of six kids, so she always felt like she had to be perfect. So she bottled everything up, and her emotions just boiled over anytime something went wrong. My sisters and I usually took the brunt of it, sometimes even physically. I worry that sometimes I let my kids get away with too much, and I think part of that is because I don't want them to feel that pressure to be perfect."

Like many of us, this woman obviously had a childhood that was less than ideal. But she can talk clearly about it, even finding compassion for her mother, and reflect on what it all means for herself and her children and even how she parents. She can offer specific details about her experience, moving easily from memory to understanding. That's a coherent narrative.

Many people grew up with parents who, while not being perfect, did a good job most of the time being consistent and predictable, and sensitively responding to their children's needs. All of this leads to secure attachment. But other people are like this mom and achieve what's called "earned secure attachment," which means that even though her parents didn't present her with the kind of childhood that would naturally lead to secure attachment, as an adult she was able to change her attachment patterns and therefore her ability to provide secure attachment to her own children by reflecting on and making sense of what she went through.

In contrast, adults who haven't done the internal work of developing a coherent narrative and earning secure attachment are more challenged in specific ways when it comes to personal insight about their past. In fact, they may have trouble even narrating their life story in a way that makes sense. When asked about their early family life, they may become lost in the details, even getting preoccupied with recent events from their adult life. Or they might not be able to recall emotional and relational details from childhood and may be cut off from an emotional life. In the most severe cases, people may have experienced so much trauma or loss as children that communication about their past becomes filled with moments of disorientation or disorganization.

Without insight and a coherent narrative that gives us a foundation for understanding ourselves and how the past has impacted who we are, it is more difficult to be fully present as a parent and to provide the type of safe, soothing communication where the child feels seen and secure. Remember the four S's (safe, seen, soothed, and secure)? That kind of presence in a child's life ultimately leads to secure attachment, the best predictor for children to thrive. When we haven't made sense of our own past, we are quite likely to repeat the mistakes of our parents as we raise our children.

But when we gather the courage to look at and get clear on our own past, and develop the insight necessary to narrate our own stories in a clear and coherent way, we can begin to

When we gather the courage to look at and get clear on our own past, and develop the insight necessary to narrate our own stories in a clear and coherent way, we can begin to heal from our past wounds.

heal from our past wounds. In doing so, we prepare ourselves to allow our children to form a secure attachment with us, and that solid relationship will be a source of resilience throughout their lives. This is one of the most important things we can do—for ourselves, for our relationships, and for our children. In effect, we are choosing to move more toward a Yes Brain for ourselves, which then becomes an inheritance we pass down to our children, and their children, and on and on.

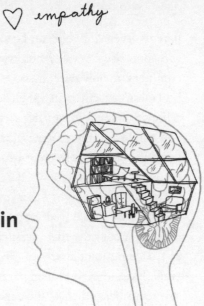

♡ empathy

CHAPTER 5

The Empathic Yes Brain

When your toddler conks you on the head with a Tinkertoy and then laughs, seemingly with no remorse, even though you are visibly hurt, it may be hard to imagine her becoming a caring, empathic person as she grows up. Or when your five-year-old puts on a cape and top hat and demands that everyone in the house stop what they are doing and sit in his audience for a spontaneous magic show that lasts and lasts and lasts (and no, you may not go to the bathroom until it's over!), his egocentrism can make you wonder if he will ever become someone who considers others.

However, we know a sixteen-year-old boy—we'll call him Devin—who consistently shows the ability to transcend self-centeredness and behave in ways that are caring and considerate. He's a typical kid with all the problems and selfishness of most teenagers: he makes irrational, teenager-esque decisions and can be way too mean to his younger sister at times. But overall, he shows the ability to care for others and compassionately consider their feelings.

Recently, for instance, on his father's birthday, Devin offered to skip an outing he had planned with his friends so he could spend time with his dad on the special day. He also regularly hugs his grandparents, even in public, and can be expected to give up his seat for someone else on a city bus without being asked. Adults regularly comment on how sweet he is.

Doesn't exactly match the clichéd image of a surly, self-absorbed, selfie-snapping teenager, does it? Based on this description of Devin, you might assume that he's just a naturally compassionate young man who was simply one of those people who are empathic from birth. But you'd be wrong.

In fact, when Devin was a young child, his parents worried about him because he showed very little innate ability to think of others' feelings or consider their perspective, even as an elementary student approaching middle school. His sister actually did seem naturally empathic and caring—her parents often had to remind her not to "overconsider" others at the expense of her own desires, and that she should stand up for herself more—but Devin clearly needed to build skills in the area of considering and caring for others. Anyone who ever disagreed with him was wrong, and he would consistently grab the first piece of birthday cake and the last remaining slice of pizza. It didn't bother him when someone else was upset, and he was, frankly, a bit of a bully to his sister and sometimes his friends at school.

But over the years Devin's parents worked with him, modeling empathy for him and using many of the strategies we'll discuss with you below. And now they're delighted to see that he's developed into an adolescent who shows empathy most of the time and has the potential to become a caring young adult with strong relational skills and the capacity to understand and attune to others at a fairly deep level (considering his age). He is in the process of developing the fourth Yes Brain fundamental: empathy. By helping him develop this crucial aspect of the Yes Brain, Devin's parents are giving him a powerful gift that will improve the overall quality of the rest of his life.

People who are caring and empathic are less frustrated, less angry, less judgmental—especially when their empathy leads them to act in ways that benefit the people around them. Empathy is a good example of integration in that we feel another's feelings but do not become the other person—we don't need to overidentify with the other as if that person is us. When differentiation is not maintained, empathy can feel overwhelming and even lead to burnout. Instead, the kind of empathy we are talking about emerges from integration as we retain a differentiated sense of self but openly link to another without losing that essential differentiated quality. Integration, recall, is not about blending or becoming homogenous. Integration is about balancing differentiation and linkage. People who are more empathic in this way are more invested in morals and ethics, and it's important to them to do the right thing. If they can combine their empathy with the insight we discussed in the previous chapter, the resulting mindsight will allow them to be more patient and receptive and understanding and aware, which will let them enjoy deeper and more meaningful relationships and be happier overall. Just as outward perception, through physical sight, allows us to perceive what's going on around us, mindsight with its inward perception lets us look within ourselves (using insight) or within someone else (using empathy) while having a sense of a differentiated self (integration).

And one of the most exciting realities is that, since the brain changes through repeated experiences, there are plenty of ways you can cultivate mindsight and foster empathy and caring in the lives of your children, cultivating those qualities in the everyday interactions of your family by strengthening the circuits of the brain that give rise to empathy. Those circuits emerge from various parts of the brain—scientists talk about limbic resonance that proceeds from the downstairs brain as well as cortical understanding and compassion originating in the upstairs brain. And you can provide your kids with opportunities that foster the growth and development of these crucial parts of their brains.

Is My Child Too Selfish?

Lots of parents feel concerned when they see in their kids selfish traits similar to the ones Devin's parents saw in him when he was younger. They want to raise children who are invested in the well-being of others, ones who are kind and compassionate, so it troubles them when they witness seemingly self-serving and unfeeling characteristics in their little ones.

When parents express these concerns to us, we remind them that the main part of the brain responsible for empathy is still particularly undeveloped in young children, and that empathy and caring—like the other fundamentals of the Yes Brain—are skills to be learned. Just as we saw with Devin, kids can develop the ability to consider and care for others. We'll explain more fully, but first we want to caution you about unnecessarily globalizing any egocentrism you might be perceiving in your kids at the moment. In other words, be careful about overreacting to what seems a lack of empathy in your young children.

For example, it may be that you simply haven't given development time to occur. In truth, it's developmentally typical for children to consider themselves first; it gives them a better chance of surviving. But from time to time we'll get parents in our offices who say something like, "I think my child is a sociopath. She's just so narcissistic and selfish. She shows no capacity at all to think about anyone other than herself." We'll then ask, "How old is your daughter?" and we'll hear, "Three." At this point we just smile and assure the parents that it's a bit early to begin worrying about a life of crime, and there's no reason yet to Google the phrase "best prisons for family visiting hours." They first simply need to let development do its job.

Or sometimes parents will notice a shift where their usually generous and compassionate child seems to become more self-absorbed, and they'll worry that it's the beginning of a trend toward a lack of empathy. In these cases, we first explore with the parents whether it could just be a phase the child is going through, and what needs the child might be communicating. We remind them that their child's brain and body are changing rapidly, and that those changes necessarily alter behavior and perspective. We also check out any transitional life events—minor or major—that could be impacting the child: a tooth comes in, a cold comes on, the family moves, a sibling is born. Also, growth spurts—physical, cognitive, motor—can cause other areas of development to regress. Transitions and surprises keep parents from ever really having a handle on it all. Human development isn't predictable and linear; it's more of a "two steps up, one step back" kind of thing, and sometimes it's upside down and sideways. That means that even if we were able to figure out the "correct answer" for responding to this particular phase, things would shift as soon as we solved the riddle anyway. So the fact that your child has appeared more selfish than usual lately isn't quite evidence that her character has developed some sort of major flaw that will prevent her from ever expressing compassion for the rest of her life.

In fact, while we're on this subject, let us remind you of one important truth that we try to keep in mind ourselves: in your role as a parent, *right now* is all you have to focus on. Yes, you are building skills to last a lifetime, it's true. But the only way you do that is in this present moment, right now. You don't have to let the experience of right now make you fret about what your child will be like at age fifteen or twenty. You really don't. *So much* development will unfold between now and then. These Yes Brain skills are set up for you to support now, and they will become skills of the future as time unfolds. Even though we're professionals who have rigorously studied development, we've been surprised at developmental leaps our respective children have made at times in just weeks and months! So don't give in to the temptation to worry that any phase—whether the concern is selfishness, sleep problems, bed-wetting, tantrums, homework meltdowns, or something else—will last forever. Your daughter won't be biting her friends when she leaves for college. (If she is, you should probably call us.) She won't have a hard time sitting at a dinner table. And she won't be oblivious to the feelings and desires of the people around her. Instead of fearing and fretting about lifelong problems, think in smaller chunks of time, maybe semesters or seasons. If you like books, think in terms of paragraphs, pages, and chapters. Give your child a few months to work through this phase,

In your role as a parent, *right now* is all you have to focus on.

this chapter of her life, and know that as long as you're there loving her, guiding her, teaching her, and providing a consistent presence in her life, she'll get through it and learn the skills she needs in order to thrive.

Our point here, in other words, is that even when you're not observing the caring, considerate, loving characteristics you'd like to see in your kids, resist the temptation to make some sort of fatalistic pronouncement about their character for all eternity. Instead, remind yourself that there's a lot of development to occur over the coming years, and then focus your efforts on helping to give your kids skills that will lead them toward being more caring and empathic. Naturally that *is* about the future, skills that will be available to them as they grow, but the only thing to focus on is what's happening right in this present moment. The interactions you have right now are the place where learning happens. Remember, *behavior is communication*. When we see behaviors that we don't like, those actions are actually telling us, "Help! I need skill-building in this area!"

If your child was struggling with his multiplication tables, you'd want to give him more math practice. Likewise, if you notice that empathy seems to be lacking, give him opportunities to build a more caring brain. These skills can be built.

One quick caveat about what empathy is *not*: it's not about learning to please others at the expense of one's self. Some kids are like Devin's sister, whose parents had to regularly remind her to stand up for herself. They repeatedly told her that it's okay to say no and to ask for what she wants. We don't want to create kids who grow into people-pleasers unsure of their own desires and unable to take care of themselves. We simply want them to care about and remain aware of how other people feel, rather than catering to every opinion and demand made by someone in their life.

Likewise, recall that empathy has many dimensions and isn't *just* about understanding the perspective of another person. Plenty of

Behavior Is Communication

The behavior we see:

What's really being communicated:

politicians and salespeople are skillful in this area and use those abilities to manipulate others. That's why when we teach empathy, we stress that it's not just about *understanding* how others feel and what they want, but about developing a brain that actually *cares* for other people. It's about discovering how *interconnected* we all are.

Each of us, after all, is a unique, self-contained individual: a *me*. But we also affect and are affected by one another. The people in our lives are a part of us, and we're a part of them. All of us make up a collective "we." *Empathy allows us to keep in mind that each of us is not only a "me," but part of an interconnected "we" as well.* Recognition of this combination—Dan calls it "MWe"—helps produce an integrated self that leads not only toward caring for others, but also toward living a life full of meaning, connection, and belonging to a larger whole.

The Empathy Diamond

There are actually many different facets of empathy, as we've seen. A common definition focuses on feeling with another person or sensing another's experience, then caring about what that person is going through. This is what Atticus Finch, from *To Kill a Mockingbird*, was talking about when he said that we never really understand someone until we "climb into his skin and walk around in it." That's a great description of empathy.

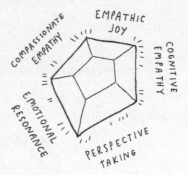

But we can be more detailed than that. We like to talk about the "empathy diamond," which represents the five facets of empathy and the many different ways we can care for others and respond to their pain:

> *Perspective taking*: Seeing the world through the eyes of another
> *Emotional resonance*: Feeling the feelings of another
> *Cognitive empathy*: Understanding, or intellectually getting, another's overall experience
> *Compassionate empathy*: Sensing suffering and wanting to reduce it
> *Empathic joy*: Experiencing delight with the happiness, achievements, and well-being of another

Taken together, the facets of empathy explain what it means to truly feel with someone, then also take action to help. When we serve others and become a change-maker in the world, we live out of an authentic morality. Empathy, in other words, directly leads us to make moral and ethical decisions, since if we care for someone, we're much less likely to lie to him, for example, or to steal from him, or to oppress him in some way.

Somewhat ironically, acting in the interest of others can also promote self-care. After all, when we repeatedly sense others' pain and distress without acting to alleviate it, we can experience empathy fatigue and burnout. But studies show that taking action to address suffering leads to increased joy. So when we talk about encouraging empathy in our kids, we want to nurture *all* the facets of the empathy diamond, including acting on someone else's behalf and helping. We want to challenge our children to be active forces in the world, which will lead to more joy in their own lives. It turns out that service to others is one of the best ways to make our own lives better as well.

Building a Brain That's Wired to Care

One of the most hopeful messages we ever give parents is that the Yes Brain skills we want to help our kids develop—about all four fundamentals, surely, and definitely about empathy—are built during normal, everyday interactions. In other words, the important parenting work is done not only when we have serious, meaningful conversations with our kids, but just as often when we simply play with them, read to them, argue with them, joke with them, or just hang out together. The science of neuroplasticity assures us that all experiences shape the brain and, for good and for bad, position children for who they'll be as they move toward adulthood.

So when it comes to empathy, lectures that begin, "You should care more about X because . . ." are rarely going to leave a lasting impression in a way that fuller experiences will. Conversations about empathy are important, of course, but much more powerful will be the example your kids see you set, and the extent to which you yourself demonstrate what it means to listen to others, consider their perspectives and opinions, and care about them. That kind of modeling, particularly how you show compassion *for them* when they are having a hard time, will help your children build their capacity for empathy. And when they watch you make an effort to live a life full of concern for the people around you and an awareness of others' needs, your kids will assume that's just how things are done, and empathy will become more of their automatic, default approach to the world.

But building a caring brain goes beyond merely teaching about empathy, or even modeling it. Kids learn empathy by experiencing it and feeling the internal satisfaction and joy that come with helping someone in a meaningful way. They also learn it when they choose *not* to care about someone else and then end up feeling not so great about their decision. Most adults still remember a time in childhood when they should've helped someone and didn't, and how bad it felt; they can still feel that regret when reflecting on it. These moments are all part of building our empathy muscles. The goal is to help wire our kids' brains in such a way that it orients them, at a deep level, to other people and their feelings. We want to engage our children's neural circuitry in a manner that encourages them to think about and feel concern for the people around them, and to do the right thing. We want to nurture a brain that's wired to care—about others, and about right and wrong.

The goal is to help wire our kids' brains in such a way that it orients them, at a deep level, to other people and their feelings. We want to engage our children's neural circuitry in a manner that encourages them to think about and feel concern for the people around them, and to do the right thing. We want to nurture a brain that's wired to care—about others, and about right and wrong.

How do we do that beyond talking with them about empathy and modeling it for them? We can draw their attention to the needs of the people around them. Repeated attention given to any experience or set of information activates neurons and strengthens their connections. We want to stimulate neuronal activation and growth. We want to SNAG a child's brain in the area of empathy.

Stimulate

Neuronal

Activation and

Growth

Remember, where attention goes, neurons fire. And where they fire, they wire. This is how connections across the brain are distributed, and therefore how integration occurs. So when we give our kids experiences that draw their attention to other perspectives and the concerns of other individuals, we SNAG their brains for empathy, because that attention causes neurons to fire and to wire together in ways that promote future empathy as well.

That's what Devin's parents did when he was younger. They spent time drawing his attention to other people's experiences and minds and helping him consider the feelings of others, thus encouraging and strengthening synaptic connections that eventually resulted in his developing a true sense of empathy, so much on display as a sixteen-year-old. When they read to him they asked questions like "What is the Lorax feeling right now? Why is he so mad at the Once-ler for chopping down all the trees?" When they watched movies, they would occasionally pause the film to ask questions like "Why do you think Travis got sad when Old Yeller started acting so differently? What do you think he should do? What's the right thing here?" Simply by drawing awareness to characters' emotions and motivations, they helped Devin move outside of himself and realize that the people on the pages and the screen had their own subjective interests and considerations that were quite apart from his own.

From there it was easy enough to ask similar questions about the lives of real people: "Ms. Azizi got upset more easily than usual during class today, huh? I wonder what might have happened to her this morning before school?" In simple conversations during normal, everyday interactions, basic questions—"Why do you think Ashley is feeling sad? How can we help?"—build the scaffolding for an in-

Empathy is a Yes Brain skill, and a caring brain can be built

creased sense of mindsight, morality, and an awareness of the minds of others.

These experiences were repeated in countless conversations over the years as Devin's brain became further integrated, and he evolved from a self-absorbed child into a teenager who was usually (but not always) caring, relational, and ethical. That's the kind of reality an integrated brain produces. Integration made visible is kindness and compassion.

Integration made visible is kindness and compassion.

The other decision Devin's parents made to help guide him toward being more empathic was to allow him to experience his own negative emotions. As you've heard us stress repeatedly throughout the book, the point is *not* to create a version of your child that *you* want to see develop, but to allow each individual child to develop into him- or herself. Building an empathic brain is about giving your kids more skills, not turning them into who you want them to be.

We've talked a good bit so far about the problems that result from overprotecting kids, which keeps them from learning the lessons and resilience that come with disappointment, frustration, and even defeat. Bubble-wrapping kids also prevents the full development of empathy, which often emerges directly from having experienced negative emotions themselves. Each time Devin's parents allowed him to feel sad or frustrated or disappointed, instead of immediately distracting him or rushing in to fix things, his potential for empathy grew, since his own struggles opened up space within him to understand and identify with the pain of others. His parents sat with him and supported him in his pain, of course, but they didn't deny or distract him from his feelings, since they knew how important, instructive, and even healthy negative emotions can be.

When he was very young this might have meant simply holding him for an extra minute or two while he cried when his grandmother left town, rather than immediately offering to bake cookies to get his mind off his sadness. As he grew older and faced bigger disappointments, like the time in middle school when he was abandoned by two of his friends on a field trip and had to sit on the bus alone, it meant listening to his fears that everyone at school hated him and that he'd be friendless forever. At times like these his parents were tempted to try to move him immediately back into happiness and offer suggestions, but instead they did their best to first lovingly listen and allow him to know what emotional pain feels like. They said things like, "That sounds like it felt really lonely. You're worried about friends beyond what happened on the field trip today. This is really hard."

Then, once he had expressed himself and was receptive to talking about his experience, they could explain that when he feels emotional pain it isn't fun, but it can help him understand and care for others who are feeling lonely or worried. They could also then problem-solve and ask more questions about the situation, but only after allowing him to sit with his feelings.

By refusing to short-circuit Devin's emotional process by rescuing from him from negative feelings, they helped further develop the Yes Brain capability of empathy and move him toward becoming a caring adolescent and, one day, an adult with great capacity to participate in meaningful relationships.

The Science of Empathy

Over the last few years, scientists have delved much more deeply into empathy, and it becomes more and more clear that the human brain is wired for caring, even in very young children. Babies as young as twelve months, for example, will often attempt to soothe someone who has become upset or distressed in some way. Toddlers are justifiably known for focusing on their own needs and desires, but they also demonstrate the ability to think about and care for others, and even consider other people's feelings and intentions. One study examined the interactions between a researcher and eighteen-month-olds. Once the toddler had become comfortable with the researcher, the adult would pretend to drop an object. Consistently the toddlers would crawl to the object, pick it up for the researcher, and hand it back. If, on the other hand, the adult purposely threw the object down, the toddlers were able to recognize this act of intention and therefore offered no help. They were able, in other words, to sense when the adult actually needed help. Interestingly, the researchers performed the same experiment with chimps, who proved to be much less eager to help, even if they knew the researcher and viewed him or her as a friend. They demonstrated no such empathy as exhibited by the human toddlers, who apparently have empathy and cooperation innately hardwired into their brains even at this early stage.

Fascinating research has also emerged about where empathy comes from, and how it's developed in the brain. For instance, one scientific finding that probably won't surprise you is that humans tend to be naturally egocentric. We work from what has been called an "emotional egocentricity bias" (EEB), which leads us to assume that the way we see the world is necessarily similar to how other people see it. We therefore make decisions accordingly. This tendency toward self-centeredness, when elaborated to the extreme, can lead to all kinds of problems, including narcissism, closed-mindedness, impatience, intolerance, rigidity, and an inclination toward judging and criticizing people we perceive as different from us. When we assume that our own perspective is better than or superior to or more "natural" than someone else's, we'll have a hard time viewing that person with respect and care, which of course means the two of us can't experience a meaningful relationship and will have difficulty engaging in a satisfying dialogue.

Part of growing up, then, is developing the capacity to overcome the innate and automatic tendency toward EEB. Fortunately, there's a part of the brain whose job in its role interconnecting with the overall system of the brain's circuits is to help us notice when our egocentrism is especially strong and help us adjust our thinking. It's called the right supramarginal gyrus (rSMG), and as you might expect, it resides in the upstairs brain. As one area that plays an important role in the functioning of the whole, we can see how development of the brain based on both timing and experience can shape the emergence of empathy in our kids.

The Right Supramarginal Gyrus

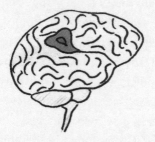

When the rSMG doesn't perform properly—or, as in the case of children, when it hasn't had time to develop—a person is more likely to project his own feelings and circumstances onto others. But the good news is that like so many other regions of the upstairs brain, a child's rSMG will continue to develop with maturity and can become more functional when the child uses it more—by repeatedly paying attention to the experiences and feelings of others. Once again, it's a skill that can be learned, an emotional muscle that can be strengthened, a part of the brain that can be developed. The more we think about and practice empathy, the more empathic we can be in the future.

A recent study made this point in a powerful fashion, examining the effects of encouraging middle-school teachers to view their students more empathically. As you may know, suspension rates in U.S. schools have been on the rise, and educational researchers have naturally been endeavoring to explain why. Some have pointed to punitive (zero-tolerance) discipline policies. Others emphasize students' lack of self-control, while still others highlight overcrowded classrooms and a lack of training for teachers.

This particular study went at the problem from a different direction. A group of teachers from five different middle schools in California were asked to complete, a couple of months apart, two online modules that asked them to think about *reasons* for student misbehavior—the challenging social dynamics in the world of young adolescents, the biological, hormonal changes taking place in their bodies and brains, and so on. The teachers learned about studies and listened to student stories that demonstrated the link between academic success, on one hand, and a safe, caring, respectful educational environment, on the other. The online modules stressed that students' emotions and behaviors improve when they feel cared about and valued by their teachers.

You can probably guess the results: compared to the control group—regardless of race, gender, family income, or even whether the students had previously been frequently in trouble—the suspension rate plummeted when teachers were asked to think about the experiences of their students. In fact, students of the teachers who participated in this "empathy training," which came at essentially no cost to the district, were *half* as likely to be suspended! Talk about real power to alter an actual problem—especially when you consider that suspension rates correlate with significant negative life outcomes, such as chronic unemployment and even prison.

So when we talk about empathy's substantial potential to affect people's lives in authentic ways, we mean it. Numerous other scientific studies have demonstrated the power of caring and empathy, not just in kids, but in adults as well. Research has found, for example, that if doctors demonstrate what's been called "clinical empathy," patients feel more respected by their practitioners and satisfied with their treatment. One study even showed that a patient with a common cold will get over the illness a day sooner and have a much more robust immune response if the physician makes an empathic comment. Beyond that, diagnoses are more accurate, overall health outcomes improve, and even malpractice claims decrease. Plus, the doctors themselves report greater job satisfaction and overall well-being.

Studies such as these across multiple domains support the power of caring for others, demonstrating that empathy can decrease aggression and behavioral problems in children, strengthen overall family and marital dynamics, and reduce sexual assaults and domestic violence. Science, in other words, strongly supports what you've likely witnessed in your own life and in the life of your kids: that caring for others and working hard to remain aware of other perspectives can lead to all kinds of positive outcomes and improve the meaning and significance we experience in our lives.

One way to understand the power of this fourth facet of the Yes Brain is that empathy is a powerful way that we can create that important experience of integration in our lives. With empathy, we remain differentiated but attain a crucial linkage to others: we share our internal, subjective feelings with another person, and two separate individuals become a part of a "we." We are social beings, and empathy is a powerful pathway to create integration in our lives. It's that simple, and simply that important.

What You Can Do: Yes Brain Strategies That Promote Empathy

Yes Brain Strategy #1 for Promoting a Caring Brain: Fine-Tune the "Empathy Radar"

One of the best ways to help kids care for others is to activate their brain's social engagement system in such a way that they're prepared to view situations through the lens of empathy and caring for others. We call this fine-tuning your kids' empathy radar.

An active empathy radar helps children notice and attune to other people's minds so they can pick up signals, both verbal and nonverbal. It's a bit like emotional mind-reading. It might mean simply being more aware of times when they're dominating a conversation, or finding ways to be polite and get along, even when they're in a bad mood. Or it might mean recognizing when someone *else* (like maybe their tired parent!) is in a bad mood, then deciding to be more sensitive or to be more careful about pushing the other person's buttons. When the empathy radar is activated, we become more mindful and more receptive to understanding another person's state of mind. From this mindful place we can be much better at monitoring given situations for ways we can help make the people around us happier, or relieve their distress in some way—again, while maintaining an appropriate level of self-care along the way.

There are lots of ways you can develop this mindfulness in your children and help turn on their empathy radars. For example, as we discussed in Chapter 4, you can reframe situations for them by encouraging curiosity. Help them learn to be detectives and to ask different questions. When a classmate loses emotional control and runs from the playground upset, an immediate, knee-jerk reaction is to ask, "What's wrong with him?" Instead, encourage their curiosity and help them reframe the entire scenario simply by asking a different question: "I wonder why he responded like that?"

We can help our kids reframe a situation so that they're not immediately condemning and judging in anger, but instead asking questions from a place of curiosity, receptivity, and kindness. That simple act of reframing, typified in the two completely different questions, creates an entirely different experience for our kids, as well as the people in their lives.

A practical way to reframe a situation is to role-play. Say, for example, your ten-year-old comes home upset because his classmate Josh was cheating "as usual" on the handball court. You've heard this complaint about Josh numerous times, so you decide to try something new and role-play with your son. You tell him, "I'll be you, and you be Josh." Then, playing the role of your son, you might say, "Josh, you were totally cheating at handball. You know you can't hit the ball twice in a row, and you did. Then you said that one shot was out, when it was really on the line."

Most likely, your son won't know how to respond as Josh, other than to say, "No it wasn't." Eventually, though, by pushing him to go

Engage the Empathy Radar

Instead of judging . . .

Teach kids to use their curiosity

deeper, you can challenge him to see *why* Josh so often takes liberties with the rules. Your son might ultimately say, still pretending to be Josh, "I just never win at anything, so that's why I cheat sometimes." Or maybe he'll think about what he knows about Josh's parents. Maybe his father frequently quotes Vince Lombardi—"Winning isn't everything, it's the only thing"—which creates an overcompetitiveness within Josh and leaves him feeling like it's unacceptable to lose. Again, it may require plenty of direction and prompting from you to help your son come to these insights, and it doesn't have to all feel perfectly natural. But simply by helping him take Josh's perspective, you will give your son the opportunity to practice some emotional mind-reading and realize that there are probably reasons beneath Josh's behavior, which can create more forgiveness now and more patience in the future. (This is a good way for us to approach our own children's behavior as well.)

Sometimes the best way to heighten the sensitivity of your children's empathy radars is simply to bring attention to situations where victims, or outsiders of any kind, need support. The classic example in the childhood realm is the one where someone is being bullied. You can offer hypothetical situations, or maybe your child knows of an actual bullying dynamic from her school. For most kids it won't take much effort to sympathize with the victim. One simple question can get them there: "What do you think it's like for her being picked on all the time?" Then you can lead them in a discussion of how best to respond when someone is being intimidated or mistreated in some way. The same goes for circumstances when a child is being made fun of, left out, or treated cruelly in any other way. Simply helping your kids consider how it feels to be in that particular position will go a long way toward engaging the radar.

And again, this kind of empathy-promotion can occur through your routine interactions with your kids. Sometimes you might initiate a more serious conversation about empathy. But more often, you'll just use typical daily situations to offer repeated opportunities for thoughtfulness. We know a grandmother, for example, who often watches her grandchildren. At bedtime each night, they all go through their "Peace Be's" together. They say, "Peace be to my friend Katinka, who seemed sad at school today," or "Peace be to those people without clean water." Asking kids to brainstorm with you and consider all the hands that were involved in getting food onto their plates for dinner is another nice way to think beyond ourselves. The very act of considering other people's experiences opens up whole new opportunities to engage our empathy radar.

Birthdays and other holidays also give kids the chance to think about the desires of others. One current trend we've noticed at birthday parties, especially as kids get older, is to simply give a gift card to the birthday boy or girl. There's certainly nothing wrong with this trend, but it doesn't offer the same opportunity that traditional gift-giving offers, where a child has to consider and choose what a friend might want or enjoy. The same goes for presents for a grandparent or aunt or uncle. It's much easier to buy something yourself and have everyone sign the card. But having the kids pick out a present, then create a homemade card with construction paper and glue, allows them to consider what will make another person happy. Doing so greatly increases the sensitivity of the empathy radar.

Yes Brain Strategy #2 for Promoting a Caring Brain: Establish a Language of Empathy

Another way to build empathy is to provide kids with a vocabulary they can use to communicate that they care for others. After all, even when children *can* take the perspective of others and identify with their feelings, they often haven't developed the ability to communicate that empathy. So we teach them.

Sometimes this means introducing them to the basics of effective emotional communication, such as listening well before ever offering advice when someone is hurting. And it might mean teaching them tried-and-true techniques such as "speaking from the I," where we focus on how "I" feel, rather than what "you" did to me. It's much

Teach kids that blaming and criticizing . . .

Causes more problems than "speaking from the I"

more effective to say "I feel mad when you don't put the crayons back" than to say "You're always losing the crayons."

Apologies are similar. When your daughter pushes her little

brother into the pool, "I'm sorry" is fine. But it shows more care and concern to teach her to address her brother's feelings. In her own words she might say some version of "I thought it would be funny, but I know you didn't get a chance to take a breath before going underwater. I know that was scary, and I shouldn't have done that." Helping her develop a language of empathy will not only help her communicate in a more caring way, but SNAG her brain for empathy as well.

One of the most important language-of-empathy skills we can give children has to do with how to communicate love when someone is hurting. We want to help our children notice when others are in pain, and also show them how they can respond in caring ways. For very young children, the goal is often just to help them join with another. A humorous example of this joining occurred when Andrew, a friend of Tina's three-year-old son, Ben, mentioned that his dog had just died. Ben commiserated by telling Andrew that his two fish, Gitchigoomee and Pirate Pirate, had recently died as well. Ben was then quiet for a moment, clearly trying to put together a few details and remembering how he and his mom had flushed the dead fish. Then he asked, "Does your house have a really big toilet?"

One of the best things about children is this willingness to join with another person's experience. As they mature, they develop the desire to help in more meaningful ways. Their immediate inclination will often be the same as ours: to offer advice when someone is hurting ("You should just . . ."), or to try to mitigate the pain and help them see the bright side ("At least you have another dog"). These well-meaning responses are evidence that our kids care, and we should praise them for their good motives. But we want to teach them that empathy is rarely about giving advice or finding a silver lining. It's much more about listening, being present, and sharing feelings. We want to teach them phrases like "That must really hurt" and "I don't know what to say, but I'm sorry this happened."

As we teach about the language of empathy, we do have to be careful about expecting too much, from kids of any age. After all,

Teach kids that giving advice . . .

Isn't as powerful as listening and being present

even adults can have a hard time effectively expressing their feelings when they're upset. But with practice, even very young children can develop the ability to use basic empathic conversational skills. And when children develop even a rudimentary language of empathy, they prepare themselves for much deeper relationships and create the scaffolding that will allow them to live richer and more meaning-ful relational lives as they grow into adulthood.

Yes Brain Strategy #3 for Promoting a Caring Brain: Expand the Circle of Concern

When we talk about building a caring brain, we often think about teaching kids to care for the people in their lives: family, friends, other kids at school, and so on. But as important as it is to remain aware of the desires and needs of those around us, true empathy goes beyond caring for those we already know and love. A caring brain works to expand its "circle of concern," increasing its awareness and understanding of people outside its immediate and most intimate connections.

There are all kinds of ways we expand a child's circle of concern. Once again, it largely comes down to simply exposing kids to the internal worlds of others—making them aware of what they may or may not be noticing on their own. When your region experiences a heat wave, talk to your kids about how thirsty homeless people might get, and how many people suffer greatly because they don't have air-conditioning. Then think together about who those people are and brainstorm together about ways you might help. Or when it snows, think about any neighbors who might need help shoveling sidewalks or getting to the store. Most kids love the opportunity to help others if we can just guide them to recognize the needs of the people around them.

Volunteering and community service are powerful ways to intro-duce your kids to the struggles others in the world face. If you're wor-ried that your children are growing up in a self-contained bubble that shields them from real knowledge about pain and suffering, then visit or volunteer together at a homeless shelter, retirement center, or hospital. As always, be cognizant of each child's age and stage of de-velopment, and don't expose them to more than they can handle. But one of the best ways for kids to recognize and care about others' pain is to witness it for themselves. And once the light of awareness comes on, it can begin to grow and shine of its own accord.

You can also expand your children's circle of concern by expressing interest in activities that include people from backgrounds different from your own. That might entail simply signing up for sports and other activities that allow your children to interact with kids from various and diverse communities and neighborhoods. Then you can all meet people from outside your bubble. Or most cities have pockets of international communities. Visit restaurants, libraries, or places of worship, meeting the people there. Enter not as tourists visiting an exotic locale, but as fellow humans open to learning and appreciating other ways to interact with the world.

There's no single right way to expand your children's circle of concern. The point is simply to watch for opportunities to open your children's eyes to the perspectives and needs of other people—both the people they know and the ones whose lives they might not have thought about without your help.

Yes Brain Kids: Teach Your Kids About Empathy

Again, building a caring brain begins with helping children step beyond their own individual perspectives and consider what someone else is experiencing. We've found it effective to teach kids about "seeing with their heart."

Yes Brain Kids: In the other "Yes Brain Kids" sections we've talked a lot about paying attention to your own reactions, and what's going inside you. Now we want to talk about seeing what's going on inside someone else.

When you look at a friend, you can see what she looks like on the outside. And if you have an X-ray, you can see the inside of her body.

But did you know you can look at someone with your heart, too? That happens when you notice how that person is feeling, like whether she's happy, or sad, or angry, or excited.

When you use your heart to look at someone, you pay attention to his face, but also his body. Can you tell how this boy feels, just from looking at his body language?

That's Carter. And if you said he looks sad, you're right. He's sad because a bigger boy at school was mean to him and pushed him down.

Carter never told Lottie he was sad, but when she looked with her heart, she could tell. She could see her brother's feelings, and her heart hurt.

Since she had looked at her brother with her heart, Lottie knew she needed to check on him. She asked about his feelings, and the two kids decided to ask their mom for advice about the bully.

The next time someone around you is hurting, look with your heart. Pay attention to what that person is feeling. If you can just notice what's going on inside that other person, you'll probably know just what to do.

My Own Yes Brain: Promoting Empathy in Myself

We talked above about giving kids a language of empathy that allows them to communicate care and concern for others, which will then further deepen their ability to love and empathize with people who are hurting. Now we want to introduce you to a way for you, the adult, to think about responding when people in your life face a challenging situation. The crucial concept is that you can retain a differentiated sense of being you, while also reaching out to receive the feelings of another. Integration is at the heart of compassionate empathy, and research reveals that when we reach out to help others rather than overidentify with their pain as our own, we can retain a sense of equlibrium while caring compassionately for others. Emotional resonance that loses differentiation can lead to burnout and a shutting down that both depletes us and makes us unavailable to help others.

An important part of "promoting empathy in myself," then, is cultivating empathy *for* yourself. What we mean by this is what researchers call "self-compassion," the way we can learn to be kind to ourselves—to be supportive rather than harsh. When we role-model this kindness toward ourselves in our own actions, we teach our children how to be this way toward themselves.

Having empathy toward oneself is about a positive attitude, not having a lack of discipline or low standards of expectations. Think of how you might communicate with your own best friend. You'd listen to her in an open, mindful way, suspending judgment and trying to simply be present and receptive for what she was saying. You'd show her kindness and compassion, wouldn't you? Kindness can be viewed as honoring someone's vulnerability and doing something to support him while not expecting anything in return. Compassion is the way we sense another's suffering, think of how to help him feel better, and then take action to help reduce his suffering. And we might even say to our friend who's made a mistake something like, "Oh, that's something I did, too," or "That's just what people do sometimes."

The researcher Kristin Neff identifies three crucial aspects of self-compassion: being mindful, being caring, and being aware of being a part of a larger humanity. As you cultivate these elements of empathy for yourself, you'll be creating the inner kindness and compassion that you can teach to your child, too. And wouldn't you want your child's relationship with herself to be as caring and supportive as it would be with her own BFF? That's a Yes Brain way to create empathy toward oneself that lasts a lifetime.

Rethinking Success: A Yes Brain Perspective

hen you think about what success in life means for your kids, what do you have in mind? We've argued throughout the book for what we can call Yes Brain success, based on helping our children stay true to who they are while guiding them as they build skills and abilities that allow them to interact with the world from a place of balance, resilience, insight, and empathy. This authentic success occurs when kids develop an open and receptive approach to their experiences, so that they welcome new opportunities and challenges, prize curiosity and adventure, and come out on the other side of adversity with a fuller understanding of themselves, their strengths, and their passions.

But let's be real here. This is not the definition of success that guides much of contemporary culture. Many parents and schools are driven by a very different notion of success—one usually measured not from the inside out, but from the outside alone. Filled with a sense of imminent failure and inadequacy, the societal and school settings we have created in modern times often fill children and adolescents with a rigid, fear-based, No Brain state that leaves them saying, "What I *do*, what I *accomplish* and *achieve*, are the only valid measures of my worth." This is No Brain thinking because it rigidly shuts down any openness to alternative or exploratory perspectives that might modify not only the journey, but the destination itself. It results in neither balance nor resilience, neither insight nor empathy.

Our disagreement with that kind of No Brain thinking is *not* that it leads automatically to failure. In fact, a focus on external achievement can even produce a great deal of outwardly measured "success," especially if we evaluate success as so many do these days: by good grades, athletic and artistic accomplishments, and popularity with teachers and other adults. These external measures of success, these visible goals, can result in this type of achievement because they make such a heavy investment in following the rules and coloring inside the lines, rather than taking risks and trying something new as we discover who we really are and what provides us with joy and satisfaction in life. Rigidly adhering to convention and the status quo is often the most certain way to earn gold stars from teachers and other authority figures.

But obviously, gold stars aren't our highest goal for our kids. In other words, our central aim is *not* to help them become good at pleasing others, especially when that means missing out on the meaning and excitement that come from exploration, imagination, curiosity, and all the adventurous aspects of the Yes Brain. *Of course* we want our kids to do well in school and in their various activities, just as we want to teach them the social skills to get along with others and be comfortable in a multitude of situations. But ultimately, gold stars and pleasing others aren't what life's about—whether we're talking about hypercompetitive kids at elite prep schools or underserved students just trying to survive in an educational system where they feel lost and abandoned. That kind of extrinsic motivation isn't what we want our children basing their most essential decisions on.

Wouldn't we rather have our kids discover who they are, and find out what matters most to them and what makes them fulfilled, what gives them meaning, connection, and equanimity, what enables them to become authentically happy? They can still achieve great things along the way, and yes, they'll probably receive their fair share of props and accolades. But their motivation will come from *within*, rather than trying to please you or the others in their life.

How do we help our kids develop this kind of authentic, intrinsically based success in life? For us, it begins with acknowledging and honoring each child for who he or she is. Every single child has an inner spark—a combination of a unique temperament and various experiences—and we want to fan that flame to help kids become happy, healthy, and internally driven to be the "best them" they can become. The reactivity of the No Brain state shuts down curiosity and threatens to put out the flame burning within each child. The Yes Brain, in stark contrast, creates the conditions for flexibility and resilience and strength so a person's unique flame can be kindled and grow.

Eudaimonia: Honoring the Spark Within

This idea of the inner spark takes us back to the ancient Greek concept of *eudaimonia*, which referred to a life full of meaning, connection, and equanimity. The Greek word itself tells a Yes Brain story. The prefix *eu-* means "true" or "good." The term *daimon* refers to the notion that we have an authentic inner spark or self, what the writer Elizabeth Lesser describes as an inner essence, "a unique indwelling character of each person" that is "strong and luminous." As parents, we can be the guardians of our child's *daimon*, his or her unique spark. And when you combine *eu-* with *daimon*, you get *eudaimonia*, which is about the true and good life qualities that result from acknowledging and honoring our unique inner essence.

Wouldn't you like your child ultimately to experience all that comes with an awareness of that inner essence as they mature into adulthood? As Lesser puts it, "Those in touch with their authenticity share similar traits. They are gentle and strong in equal measure. They are not overly concerned about what others think of them, and yet they are greatly concerned about the well-being of others. They are so in touch with themselves that they are open toward everyone." What a beautiful description of Yes Brain success. (It's almost as if the word *eudaimonia* were Greek for Yes Brain!)

A Yes Brain approach to parenting is a way of being with each of your children that helps them develop this way of remaining in touch with their inner essence, cultivating this authentic internal compass. In Lesser's wise words, someone who has developed a strong awareness of and respect for this inner guide "feel[s] a sense of at-homeness, a lack of pretense, nothing overproduced, a wholeness." Imagine if you could set the stage in your parenting so that you could honestly offer your child this statement: "Eventually, you will come to know with all your brain cells that your authentic self is the one thing you can trust the most."

That's a Yes Brain way of giving your child the inner strength that enables a true inner guide to develop—the state of *eudaimonia*. It's not that the inner spark is a *fixed* entity; there's not one inner essence within each of us that never changes. Instead, the point here is about embracing the notion that one can live with an internal focus of motivation and a sense of respect for the inner, authentic *experience* of being alive. This connection to a true and authentic inner essence, this living with *eudaimonia*, is filled with meaning, connection, and equanimity in life. Meaning is about having a sense of what really matters. Connection is being in open communication with others, and yourself. And equanimity is the ability to achieve emotional equilibrium, to have a full range of emotions and attain a sense of balance within that rich inner and interpersonal life that both creates and embraces who we are and who we can become.

This Yes Brain approach helps develop the kind of successful life that prepares our kids from the inside out, giving them a deep awareness of inner processes that will serve as a guiding compass to know their own sense of meaning and values. It's about valuing the inner journey rather than focusing on the ultimate destination. It's about prizing process over endpoint and encouraging disciplined effort and exploration, not just outwardly measurable achievements. And none of that can happen if we impose on our kids a one-size-fits-all definition of success. Instead, we need to help them figure out who they are so that they can not only succeed, but succeed in a way that emerges from and matches their talents and desires.

> We need to help our kids figure out who they are so that they can not only succeed, but succeed in a way that emerges from and matches their talents and desires.

Redefining Success

Think about your own children right now. What do you ultimately want for them? All parents hope their kids are happy and successful, but what does that actually mean? There's nothing wrong with the extrinsic rewards of gold stars (in the form of good grades, musical awards, athletic accomplishments, and so on). But we are concerned that they present a fairly limited perspective on what success really means. We've seen too many parents focus only on the concrete achievements of gold-star living, missing out on connecting with their child and cultivating the Yes Brain internal compass, leaving the child to be guided only by what *others* expect. We worry that at times missing out on Yes Brain parenting comes with a great cost.

That's why we're arguing for a broadened definition of success. Yes Brain success leaves room for external achievements and gold stars, for sure, but it's about always keeping in mind the long-term goals of developing your child's internal compass based on balance, resilience, insight, and empathy. It's ultimately about helping a child develop an integrated and connected brain so she can lead a life of rich relational connections, meaningful interactions with the world, and emotional equanimity. Put differently, a Yes Brain doesn't preclude your child from achieving success or performing well at all. But it avoids the many costs and downsides that come with the No Brain, both short-term (in the form of higher anxiety, reactivity, and the like) and long-term (in terms of less balance and resilience and self-understanding and empathy). And it focuses on the journey,

rather than on some outwardly im-
posed destination that might
not even fit in with who the
child is and what she wants.

Since you've read this
far in the book, the notion
of a Yes Brain probably
already appeals to you.
Most likely, you care a lot
about helping your children
develop a healthy sense of self,
a willingness and ability to develop strong relationships, a concern

Yes Brain success leaves room for external achievements and gold stars, but it's about much more than that. It's ultimately about helping a child develop an integrated and connected brain—a Yes Brain—so she can lead a life of rich relational connections, meaningful interactions with the world, and emotional equanimity.

for the people around them, a resilience that helps them deal with
life's inevitable pain and setbacks, and a desire to do the right thing
and live with meaning and significance and possibly even adventure.
You want, in other words, to fan the flame of their inner spark so your
kids can discover what gives them joy and fulfillment, and how they
can make the most of their distinctive gifts and abilities. That's real
success.

But we know, from parenting our own respective kids and from
talking with thousands of other parents each year, that it's easy to be
seduced by a very different definition of success. Even if you're completely committed to parenting from a Yes Brain perspective, you
may find yourself unduly influenced by peers and fears. Or you might
find yourself tempted to live vicariously through your children, be-
lieving that *their* success is your own. In many communities, performance and achievement become so highly prized that it's difficult to
stay focused on the Yes Brain principles that lead to a joyful, meaningful life. When children are very young, for example, we can easily
talk about the importance of a well-balanced lifestyle and avoiding
the overscheduling trap and allowing for plenty of down time. But as
our children grow, our better judgment can be undermined by competition, by worries that we're doing our kids a disservice by not

pushing them hard enough, by cultural norms and expectations in our neighborhood or at our kids' school. As a result, many parents— even caring, intentional parents—get stuck on the treadmill of success, forcing themselves, their kids, and the whole family to run faster and faster to keep up with some outwardly prescribed definition of true achievement.

The Treadmill of Success

Without even realizing it, many parents begin to accept vague and dubious externally based assumptions (like the one about how going to "the most elite college" will *ensure* life success), so they gradually move toward adopting similarly vague and dubious beliefs (like the one about more homework leading to more learning). Even when it puts them in debt, some parents hire private tutors and coaches, and they sign up for each new opportunity that will improve the chances of their kids being "well rounded" and accepted into one of the "right" schools. In many cases this desire directs parental decisions as soon as or even before kids begin walking and talking, at which point family life becomes dictated by structured schedules, enrichment activities, language programs, specialized training, summer school, and on and on. Whew. Talk about an exhausting, overwhelming, and even destructive treadmill! What's next? Stressfully cramming meditation classes into our kids' calendars so they can better manage the pressure they're under from the other hectically scheduled activities?

Does any of this strike a chord with you? If so, you're not alone. Parents everywhere feel overwhelmed and exhausted by a lifestyle and set of cultural values that drive them and their children relentlessly toward this very narrow definition of externally measured success. While we can certainly empathize with the initial motivation to protect our children, the sad reality is that this good intention is actually quite misguided and often leaves parents confused as to why their child is so unprepared to go out into the world with some solid sense of who they are. The treadmill pushes families and schools (as well as businesses that cater to and feed off parental fear) toward No Brain assumptions about performance and achievement that are completely out of touch with what research tells us children actually need to thrive. Some preschools are giving homework to prepare children for the rigor waiting for them in kindergarten, even though kids that age often can't yet zip up their jackets or open their string-cheese wrappers!

Numerous experts these days are decrying an epidemic of anxiety and depression among "successful" students, not to mention those who are left behind. As a result of the overemphasis on achievement and extrinsic motivation, childhood for many becomes a time of pressure and anxiety as kids work to fit into the expectations their parents and others have for them, rather than a time of free development and exploration as they discover and grow. Rather than *eudai-monia*, many experience a feeling of inadequacy even when they are at the head of their class. With only an external measure of "success" in their lives, there is a real emptiness when it comes to what has meaning and truly matters. Instead of loving to learn, feeling uplifted by education, and getting the opportunity to learn as they learn best, through play and exploration, many students today feel oppressed and overwhelmed by their experiences at school and their activities. It's a supersized focus on extrinsic motivation that impacts family life and threatens to destroy the Yes Brain and extinguish the inner spark that keeps curiosity, creativity, and a love of learning alive. We don't think it's hyperbole to say that this kind of intensity is threatening to erode childhood and a "yes" approach to living in the world.

When we talk to parents, many of them tell us they don't agree with the amount of homework their children are assigned, and they often think their kids are doing too much and feeling overwhelmed when it comes to their schedules. This frenetic, competitive need to do so much doesn't feel right to them. And research supports the notion that after a certain limited amount, this pile of homework does little except to keep kids from getting enough sleep. But parents are afraid to get off the treadmill. They're driven by fear that their child will be the only one not keeping up, not having the edge, and that feels scary because they want to do right by their kids and maximize their opportunities. As one father put it, "I've heard the research, and I'd like to back off on what I'm asking my son to do. But let's face it: I'm gambling with his future here, and that's a bet I'm not willing to make."

So in the spirit of wanting what's best for their kids, to "protect" future options, these parents continue to pack the calendar and burn the midnight oil, all in the name of "success." Ironically, they are not providing the very thing that would give their children a growth mindset and help them develop the grit to stick to challenges even during hard times. Instead of taking time to focus on a Yes Brain experience with their children, they worry that they're not offering their children "all the advantages" and assume that one of the best things they can give their kids is "mastery" over a certain skill— artistic, athletic, academic, or otherwise. As a result, there isn't time

or room for play or imagination or exploration or being in nature—
the very things, as we've been arguing, that lead to true success and
inner peace and joy.

Tina has a vivid memory from years ago when she discovered
herself in one of these rigid treadmill-of-success moments. Her two-
year-old son had become engrossed in some nesting cups on the
living-room floor just before they were to leave for a Mommy, Music,
and Me class at the YMCA. Her frustration began to grow as she realized that not only were they likely to be late for the class, but she was
also going to have to initiate the battle to extricate her son from his
game with the beloved cups.

But before waging that battle, she caught herself and laughed
about her intense drive to be punctual at an "enrichment" class for a
two-year-old who was already feeling plenty enriched by the plastic
cups. She set down her purse, slipped off her shoes, and sat on the
rug next to her son. She joined with him in his curiosity and wonder
at these magical objects that fit so perfectly within one another, and
this joining meant that the totally unnecessary battle never had to be
fought. There are times, of course, when we
can't let kids have their way. Of course
there are. One of the crucial lessons of
childhood is that we don't always get
what we want. We've made this point
repeatedly throughout the book. But
in this instance, there was no reason
for Tina to wage war with her young
son. The moments they shared on the
floor were surely worth much more than
whatever knowledge would have emerged from singing a few verses
of "Wheels on the Bus" with the other kids at the Y.

> There are times,
> of course, when
> we can't let kids have their
> way. Of course there are. One
> of the crucial lessons of
> childhood is that we don't
> always get what we
> want.

We both readily admit that there are plenty of times when we
miss opportunities like this with our own kids. All parents do. Sometimes it's because we're too busy to pay attention to what our child
needs in that moment, to join them in their interests, to explore what

they are paying attention to and share the excitement of discovery. And sometimes it's because we're working so hard to "enrich" our children that we neglect to pay attention and see what's really going on inside them, which means we're more invested in *doing* than in *being* with them or considering what they actually need. In this example Tina was able to check herself and get off the treadmill. In doing so, she earned the reward of connecting with her young son in a way she wouldn't have gotten to if she had remained committed to the schedule at the expense of fanning the flame of his innate curiosity.

Even as kids get older, there's a significant cost to dedicating childhood exclusively to hours of cello lessons, volleyball clinics, and after-school academic programs, rather than recognizing the fundamental need for kids to be allowed to be kids and just play. Their curiosities and passions often become constricted and begin to shut down, as opposed to being nourished and encouraged to continually emerge throughout childhood. Despite parents' best intentions, the extra classes and activities often end up being counterproductive for growing brains and minds, actually limiting real discovery, growth, purpose, happiness, and self-understanding. And the parents' effort often backfires in completely unforeseen ways, causing kids to hate an activity they would've been really good at and enjoyed.

Why would caring, well-intended parents act like this, as so many of us do? One reason is that external goals can be seen with our eyes; they can be measured in concrete ways. We can gain a sense of mastery, have what psychologists call agency, the source of choice and action in life, and this makes us feel empowered. With external goals, we can choose a direction, aim our children toward it, and see whether we've gotten them there or not. Internal goals—building the skills of emotional regulation and resilience; introducing an awareness of an inner world; developing the flame of desire for curiosity, compassion, and creativity; encouraging insight and a concern for others—are all inner characteristics of a child, and often less recognizable. Internal goals may be the key to social and emotional intelligence, to what creates grit and resilience, but they are harder to see with our eyes, and even harder to measure. So we often choose the easy route, jump on the external success treadmill, enter the rat race of external goal achievement, and lose sight of what we may never have even known were internal goals we could aim for.

What can be measured? A grade point average. A standardized test score. A college acceptance. These are not bad goals in and of themselves. But when they are valued over our child developing his inner compass, that's where the deep, lasting, and sometimes devastating negative consequences arise. Adolescents, for example, are more anxious, stressed, and depressed than ever before. Facing an uncertain world, having often grown up with a focus on external accomplishments and not being given the Yes Brain skills of balance, resilience, insight, and empathy, they are launched from home ill equipped to face the challenges of the world that awaits them.

Ultimately, then, we have no problem with exposing young brains to different activities and classes. Enrichment can be an important part of a child's life. Sports and music and other classes can be wonderful ways for children to develop social skills, self-discipline, and other abilities that bring them confidence and competence. Likewise, we're not at all against the importance of achievement or mastery, including doing well in school. Especially if a child is passionate about a particular pursuit, we want to encourage that desire. But there has to be a consideration of the questions "At what cost?" and "Is this for me or for my child?"

A No Brain Poster Child

Dan knows a young man—let's call him Eric—who could serve as a poster child for "No Brain success" and the drawbacks that come with it. Eric recently graduated from a top university, having jumped through all the hoops of success and checked all the achievement boxes. Before that he maintained a stellar GPA at a well-known prep school, where he starred in sports and acted in the spring musical.

Then he saw great success in college as well, graduating and immediately landing a coveted, high-paying job.

But when he recently spoke with Dan, he talked about feeling lost in terms of knowing who he really is. Despite his impressive education and imposing academic pedigree, he remains full of doubt, with plenty of self-discovery and development ahead of him. He earned plenty of gold stars along the way—he could decorate a whole corner office with them—but a sense of purpose in life has eluded him thus far.

Eric is still young and has plenty of time to discover his *daimon*, to figure out who he is and even develop a Yes Brain of his own. But what a shame that this young man with so many talents is just now beginning to ask the questions that will help develop the inner qualities so important to a life full of joy and meaning! His inner compass hasn't yet developed, and his life feels out of balance. What's more, he's missing the necessary resilience to help him weather the existential storm that's accompanying his questions regarding self and identity. At the beginning of what most would consider a more than promising career, he has no insight into whether he even wants to do this particular job, or what ideas and possibilities excite him.

In other words, whatever internal sparks were burning when he was young—whatever lit him up emotionally and intellectually— now lie dormant, waiting to be rekindled. Sadly, his parents focused only on external achievements, not on Eric's internal experience. There was little Yes Brain perspective in his parents' approach to Eric's childhood or adolescence. The fire within him was at least somewhat extinguished throughout his youth as he "achieved" and checked the appropriate boxes of apparent success. Now he's at the beginning of an adulthood bereft of *eudaimonia*. He knows how to please others, but he doesn't yet have the skills to guide himself toward what has meaning *for him*. The easily measurable external values and outcomes were prized at the expense of the internal values that lead to real and lasting personal success.

Again, there's nothing at all wrong with the "success" Eric attained. We're not campaigning against focused work, good study habits, or elite colleges. We are, however, saying that academic and career accomplishments represent only *part* of a definition of success, a narrow version that can be attained without ever developing authentic happiness and meaningful engagement in life.

What's worse, this one type of success may not at all match up with who your child really is. We all know the stereotype of the over-competitive father who forces his non-athletic son to play sports even though the child really wants to focus on music or drama. Is it any less problematic to impose an academic or career vision on a child who clearly has different goals and desires? If your child grows into an adolescent who feels passionate about succeeding at school, then by all means, honor that passion. But in doing so, remain intentional about serving a Healthy Mind Platter that achieves balance. And remain mindful of helping your child develop all the different parts of him- or herself, as well as his or her Yes Brain.

That's why we say that the parameters of concepts such as discipline, achievement, and success need to be refined to address what we now know is essential for the brain and for a child's optimal development. Contemporary research insists that true mental health, like the Yes Brain happiness and fulfillment that come with it, results not from rigid specialization, but from developing a wide array of interests and pursuits, because that kind of variety challenges and develops different parts of the brain, allowing the whole brain to grow and mature as a child's inner development occurs and different neural connections are fostered. Growth is optimized with a Yes Brain stance.

> The parameters of concepts such as discipline, achievement, and success need to be refined to address what we now know is essential for the brain and for a child's optimal development.

A Final Yes Brain Question: Are You Stoking Your Child's Inner Fire?

As you approach the closing pages of the book, take a moment now and consider how well your family's day-to-day life and interactions foster and encourage the growth of your children's Yes Brains. Ask yourself:

- Am I helping my kids discover who they are and who they want to be?
- Do the activities they participate in protect and promote their individual inner sparks? Do these activities contribute to the development of balance, resilience, insight, and empathy?
- What about our family calendar? Have I left room for them to experience moments where they can learn and explore and imagine, or do we go at such a frantic pace that they never get to relax, play, be curious, create, and just be kids?
- Am I emphasizing grades and achievement more than I should?
- Am I communicating to my children that what they do is more important than who they are?
- Is my relationship with my child being eroded by my constant pushing for him or her to do more or be better?
- What about the way my kids and I communicate about these values themselves—the things we argue about, care for, and devote time and energy to?
- In the way I communicate with my kids, am I helping their individual sparks grow, or am I diminishing them?

These are practical, Yes Brain questions we've been discussing throughout the book. Asking ourselves what we spend money on, what our calendars look like, and what we argue about most with our children can often reveal a mismatch between what we *think* we value and what we actually value. If you're like most parents, what you'll discover is that in many ways you are effectively stoking your children's inner fire, challenging them to grow and develop a robust Yes Brain. And in other ways, your family's interactions and daily life may not be supporting your kids' sparks and might perhaps even be threatening to extinguish their flame.

For us, ultimately, it's pretty simple (though not necessarily easy). Helping kids develop a Yes Brain comes down to two objectives:

1. Allowing each individual child to grow into the fullness of who he or she is, as opposed to imposing our own needs, desires, and designs.
2. Watching for times our child needs help with skill-building and developing the tools necessary to thrive.

If we can focus on these goals—honoring each child's individual flame, while also teaching him or her the skills necessary to build an internal compass and succeed in life—we will create an environment that fosters a life full of happiness, meaning, and significance. A Yes Brain life.

And after all, that's where *eudaimonia* and real success lie: in giving your kids the chance to know who they are, and to follow their desires and passions so they can live rich, full lives. Help them develop the ability to live with balance, to face adversity with resilience, to understand themselves, and to care for others. Balance. Resilience. Insight. Empathy. These are the attributes made possible by cultivating a Yes Brain. If you can support the development of these capacities in your kids, you'll be guiding them as they journey toward authentic success. They'll still face their share of struggles—we're talking about life, after all—but when they do come up against hardships, both big and small, they'll have the ability to meet them from a place of strength, with a clear sense of who they are and what they believe.

Our deepest hope is that you'll come to experience the ways a Yes

Brain parenting approach empowers you to create connections and communication with your children that support them as they develop the resilience and inner strength that will last a lifetime. With this repeated encouragement of a Yes Brain state of being in the world, your kids will develop a *eudaimonia* and an internal compass to sense their own natural proclivities that can fuel both their passion and their persistence in the face of challenges.

And that attitude is deeply reinforced when they also have a sense of purpose, one that comes from realizing, in ways that are unique to each child and that change as the different stages in their life unfold, that deep meaning and connection come from being of help to others. What a winning combination, bringing a Yes Brain approach not only to their own lives but also to their newly emerging interactions with others in the world. We hope these ideas, too, will help you cultivate such strength and an inner compass along your own parenting path ahead. Enjoy the journey!

ACKNOWLEDGMENTS

From Dan

To Tina, writing a book with you is always a pleasure, and I'd like to express my gratitude to you and Scott for your wonderful collaboration with both Caroline Welch and myself in dreaming up the ideas and ironing out the details of these various projects we engage in as a four-person team.

To my son and daughter, Alex and Maddi, now in their twenties, I am so profoundly appreciative of our connections, and for your curiosity, passion, and creativity that illuminate for me the essence of a Yes Brain approach to life.

To my life and work partner, Caroline, I am forever grateful for our relationship—a Yes Brain collaboration that continues to inspire and support me as we grow through life. As they say in Irish, It's grand to be having the *craic* (having so much fun) together!

This work would not be possible without the support, dedication, and ingenuity of our team at the Mindsight Institute: Deena Margolin, Jessica Dreyer, Andrew Schulman, Priscilla Vega, and Kayla Newcomer. I thank each of you for being a vital part of our collective efforts. Together, we endeavor to translate the interdisciplinary approach of interpersonal neurobiology into practical applications for enhancing the mindsight elements of insight, empathy, and integration that help construct the foundations of well-being in our inner and interpersonal worlds.

To my mother, Sue Siegel, who keeps us all inspired with her deep wisdom, humor, and resilience and has always been a nurturer of my own Yes Brain approach to life. And to my mother-in-law, Bette Welch, thank you for bringing such a strong and energized Yes Brain daughter into the world who is a never-ending source of vision and support for our children, for me, and for the Mindsight Institute on this wild journey of life.

From Tina

To Dan, I'm deeply honored to do this great work with you. I will always treasure you as my teacher, colleague, and friend. I'm grateful for the time that Scott and I spend with you and Caroline, and I value your friendship as much as our meaningful, fun, and productive professional partnership.

To Ben, Luke, and JP, your unique hearts, minds, senses of humor, passions, and sparks fill your dad and me and the world with so much joy. Even when life gets hard, your Yes Brains are contagious, and all three of you light me up and inspire me to say YES to the world. You make me love the world so much more.

To Scott, you *live* balance, resilience, insight, and empathy. I know our boys will be great fathers because they've learned how to do it from you. I'm grateful for your fierce love for us, and for our partnership that continues to grow. Thank you for your investment in me, in these book projects, and in our work together.

To my team at The Center for Connection, with great affection I want to thank you for teaching and inspiring me as we do the important work of curiously wrestling with complexity to help so many families: Annalise Kordell, Ashley Taylor, Allie Bowne Schriner, Andrew Phillips, Ayla Dawn, Christine Triano, Claire Penn, Deborah Buckwalter, Debra Hori, Esther Chan, Francisco Chaves, Georgie Wisen-Vincent, Janel Umfress, Jennifer Shim Lovers, Johny Thompson, Justin Waring-Crane, Karla Cardoza, Melanie Dosen, Olivia Martinez-Hauge, Robyn Schultz, Tami Millard, Tiffanie Hoang, and, finally, special thanks to Jamie Chaves for teaching me about sensory processing and the important role it plays in regulating the nervous system as we wrestled with the ideas in this book. And I'm grateful for like-minded colleagues to whom I turn for my own growth, and who lend wise minds, humor, and passion to help families and change minds about how kids work: Mona Delahooke, Connie Lillas, Janiece Turnbull, Sharon Lee, and the Momentous Institute women—Michelle Kinder, Heather Bryant, Sandy Nobles, and Maureen Fernandez.

To my parents and in-laws, Galen Buckwalter, Judy and Bill Ramsey, and Jay Bryson, you have always given me your love and support, cheering me on. My mom, Deborah Buckwalter, is the one who most modeled for me what it means to live a Yes Brain life. And I honor the memory of my dad, Gary Payne, who continues to influence me in profound ways.

From Dan and Tina

We would like to thank Doug Abrams, our literary agent, whose steady ear and loving heart provides us the space in which we can test drive our ideas and then send them out into the world. Thanks, Doug, for being passionate about our mission to share these ideas, and for being such a dear friend along this wondrous journey!

Marnie Cochran is an insightful editor who has also been supportive in the writing process from concept to text, always willing to engage with us in making the book the best form of expression we can collectively try to create. Thank you for cheering for us, joining with us, and being excited with us in this labor of love. We greatly appreciate you, Marnie.

As always, we are grateful to Merrilee Liddiard, whose talents and artistic sensibility have helped us communicate Whole-Brain, No-Drama, and now Yes Brain concepts in fuller and richer ways than mere words can do. Much gratitude to Scott Bryson for generously sharing his English Professor skills in the process. And we thank Christine Triano, Liz Olson, and Michael Thompson for the support and wise feedback they offered on early versions of the manuscript.

Our final message of gratitude is for all the parents and their children and adolescents who've been a part of our respective clinical practices and educational workshops. Thank you for being receptive and having the courage to see how the No Brain ways we can so often get stuck in can be transformed into Yes Brain freedom with effort and guidance. This book would not have been possible without the privilege we've had to be fellow travelers along this pathway toward resilience and well-being with you.

REFRIGERATOR SHEET
The Yes Brain
By Daniel J. Siegel and Tina Payne Bryson

- **Yes Brain**
  - ○ Flexible, curious, resilient, willing to try new things and even make mistakes.
  - ○ Open to the world and relationships, helping us relate to others and understand ourselves.
  - ○ Develops an internal compass and leads to true success because it prioritizes the *inner* world of a child and looks for ways to challenge the child's whole brain to reach its potential.

- **No Brain**
  - ○ Reactive and fearful, rigid and shut-down, worrying that it might make a mistake.
  - ○ Tends to focus on external achievement and goals, not on internal effort and exploration.
  - ○ Might lead to gold stars and external success, but does so by rigidly adhering to convention and the status quo and becoming good at pleasing others, to the detriment of curiosity and joy.

The Four Fundamentals of the Yes Brain

- ***Balance:* a skill to be learned that creates emotional stability and regulation of the body and brain**
  - ○ Leads to the *green zone*, where kids feel calm and in control of their bodies and decisions.
  - ○ When kids are upset they may leave the green zone and enter the revved-up, chaotic red zone, or the shut-down, rigid blue zone.
  - ○ Parents can create balance by finding the "integration sweet spot." Balance comes from being appropriately differentiated and linked.
  - ○ *Balance Strategy #1*: Maximize the ZZZ's—provide enough sleep.
  - ○ *Balance Strategy #2*: Serve a Healthy Mind Platter—balance the family's schedule.

- *Resilience:* a state of resourcefulness that lets us move through challenges with strength and clarity
  - ⊚ Short-term goal: Balance (getting back in the green zone). Long-term goal: Resilience (expanding the green zone). Both goals lead to the ability to bounce back from adversity.
  - ⊚ Behavior is communication, so instead of focusing solely on extinguishing problematic behavior, listen to the message, then build skills.
  - ⊚ Sometimes kids need pushin', and sometimes they need cushion.
  - ⊚ *Resilience Strategy #1:* Shower your kids with the four S's—help them feel safe, seen, soothed, and secure.
  - ⊚ *Resilience Strategy #2:* Teach mindsight skills—show kids how to shift their perspectives so they are not victims to their emotions and circumstances.

- *Insight:* the ability to look within and understand ourselves, then use what we learn to make good decisions and be more in control of our lives
  - ⊚ The observer and the observed: be the spectator observing the player on the field.
  - ⊚ The power is in the pause that lets us *choose* how we respond to a situation.
  - ⊚ *Insight Strategy #1:* Reframe pain—ask kids, "Which struggle do you prefer?"
  - ⊚ *Insight Strategy #2:* Avoid the Red Volcano eruption—teach kids to pause *before* erupting.

- *Empathy:* the perspective that allows us to keep in mind that each of us is not only a "me," but part of an interconnected "we" as well
  - ⊚ Like the other skills, empathy can be learned through daily interactions and experiences.
  - ⊚ It's about understanding the perspective of another, as well as caring enough to take action to make things better.
  - ⊚ *Empathy Strategy #1:* Fine-tune the "empathy radar"—activate the social engagement system.
  - ⊚ *Empathy Strategy #2:* Establish a language of empathy—provide a vocabulary that communicates care.
  - ⊚ *Empathy Strategy #3:* Expand the circle of concern—increase kids' awareness of people outside their most intimate connections.

DANIEL J. SIEGEL, M.D., is clinical professor of psychiatry at the UCLA School of Medicine, the founding co-director of the UCLA Mindful Awareness Research Center, and executive director of the Mindsight Institute. A graduate of Harvard Medical School, Dr. Siegel is the author of several books, including the *New York Times* bestseller *Brainstorm* and the bestsellers *Mindsight, Parenting from the Inside Out* (with Mary Hartzell), *The Whole-Brain Child* (with Tina Payne Bryson), and *No-Drama Discipline* (with Tina Payne Bryson). Also the author of the internationally acclaimed professional texts *The Mindful Brain* and *The Developing Mind,* Dr. Siegel keynotes conferences and conducts workshops worldwide. He lives in Los Angeles with his wife.

DrDanSiegel.com

Facebook.com/drdansiegel

Twitter: @drdansiegel

TINA PAYNE BRYSON, PH.D., is the co-author (with Daniel J. Siegel) of the bestselling *No-Drama Discipline* and *The Whole-Brain Child*. She is a pediatric and adolescent psychotherapist, the Director of Parenting for the Mindsight Institute, and the Child Development Specialist at Saint Mark's School in Altadena, California. She keynotes conferences and conducts workshops for parents, educators, and clinicians all over the world. Dr. Bryson earned her Ph.D. from the University of Southern California, and she lives near Los Angeles with her husband and three children.

TinaBryson.com

Twitter: @tinabryson

Find Tina Payne Bryson on Facebook

ABOUT THE TYPE

This book was set in Minion, a 1990 Adobe Originals typeface by Robert Slimbach (b. 1956). Minion is inspired by classical, old-style typefaces of the late Renaissance, a period of elegant, beautiful, and highly readable type designs. Created primarily for text setting, Minion combines the aesthetic and functional qualities that make text type highly readable with the versatility of digital technology.